Gateway to Forgiveness and Beyond

Gateway to Forgiveness and Beyond

Radhi Al-Mabuk
Len Froyen

© 2018 Radhi Al-Mabuk, Len Froyen
All rights reserved.
ISBN-13: 9781983568060 (CreateSpace-Assigned)
ISBN-10: 1983568066

Dedication "We gratefully dedicate this book to our parents, spouses, and children who taught and inspired us to stand inside the meaning and purpose of forgiveness and to foresee, trust and facilitate its peacemaking possibilities."

Table of Contents

	Said About Book Perspective and Practice	ix
	Preface	1
	Introduction	4
Chapter One	Our Origins	12
Chapter Two	Forgiving is Unnatural	23
Chapter Three	Revenge is Natural	37
Chapter Four	Gateway One: Awareness of the Injury	53
Chapter Five	Gateway Two: Experience the Pain	67
Chapter Six	Gateway Three: Dealing With the Pain	78
Chapter Seven	Gateway Four: Making the Decision to Forgive	91
Chapter Eight	Gateways Five & Six: Forgiveness Tools	104
Chapter Nine	An Interlude	123
Chapter Ten	From Forgiveness to Reconciliation	131
Chapter Eleven	Beyond Forgiveness & Reconciliation: Becoming a New Creation	153
	Bibliography	191
	Authors' Biographies	199

Said About Book Perspective and Practice

WHAT THE AUTHORS would like you to know about this book. It is:

- devoted to a topic that has been gaining considerable attention in both popular and academic literature.
- written for those who have not found relief by avoiding their pain of unforgiving relationships.
- a concise, honest and trusting step-by-step journey of forgiveness, that will eventuate greater emotional health and freedom.
- based on a comprehensive forgiveness model that has been empirically and extensively investigated.
- a useful tool for helping professionals such as counselors, psychotherapists, social workers, alternative health educators, and pastors.
- a potential resource for forgiveness studies courses and allied areas such as peace studies, conflict and stress management, and mental health.
- a bridge to the generative process of reconciliation and character formation.
- written in a clear, sensitive, and image-rich style that is equally appealing to laypersons and professionals.

It is anchored in a resolution strategy for decreasing negative emotions such as anger, resentment, rage, hate and shame; reduction in emotional states like anxiety, depression, loneliness, alienation, and despair; and the restoration of fractured or broken relationships. The field of forgiveness has been growing as attested by the number of books devoted to various aspects of the topic. Our work takes a practical approach to all the steps involved in the process of forgiving.

Preface

WE ARE ALL born into a relationship. Our parents are our first and foremost connection to all other relationships. We depend upon them to provide the sustenance to feed our body and the concepts to structure our mind. They make the world livable and order it for us. We learn to trust them because they are an essential connection to all that is life and all that is life-giving. Trust is the linchpin that holds everything together and helps us feel secure in an ever-demanding and ever-changing world.

But, our parents are not perfect. They are not always a reliable interpretation of the world or a dependable provision for our needs. Even when they have good intentions, at times they lack the foresight, the ability, or the skill to do the right thing. We learn they cannot always be trusted to provide what we need or give us what we want. We begin to look elsewhere when we no longer feel confidently secure and satisfied with what they do or offer. However, we find other people are also imperfect. They may even be less dependable and reliable than our parents. Our well-being is less likely to be their concern and the basis for their commitment. They are even less trustworthy and lacking in their ability or desire to address our needs and wants.

People and life often let us down. I cannot always count on life to simply give me what I want and for people to do as I like. I find myself resenting this lack of correspondence between having trusted and now feeling abandoned when I am down in the dumps and down on life. There is nothing quite like counting on something or someone and being disappointed because things didn't work out or someone failed to be reliable and responsible.

We can despair of this situation, or we can work to alleviate the conditions that precipitated it. We can be fatalistic and die to those who hung us out to dry and left us swinging in the wind. Or, we can acknowledge that we live in an imperfect world with imperfect people. With this latter attitude, we can work to undo the hard feelings and hardships that are an inevitable aspect of all relationships. We learn to make allowances for good intentions that have gone awry. Although we feel wronged, rather than dwelling on the hurt, we look for a cure. We learn expectations can make us hostages of disappointment. We learn there will seldom be a one-to-one correspondence between what we want and what we get. No one person is at fault, no one condition is to blame, nor will one solution satisfy our longing to be whole. We learn most people are working to do the best they can. We might be surprised at how well they do if we knew all the circumstances of their lives. No one gets up in the morning, sits on the edge of the bed, and says, "I am going to be unbelievably obnoxious and dutifully bad today." We set out to do the best we can because that is the way we are constructed. We <u>can</u> learn to be generous and give others the benefit of the doubt. At least the doubt can open the door we often shut in another's face—the door we refuse to open for fear of what we might encounter on the other side.

Trusting something else, trusting someone else, is the first step in building and rebuilding relationships. Trust entitles us to do things over and make things right. Trust is a risk we take because we believe the essence of life requires an investment in people. We have to spend something and save something to feel secure and grow whole in our relationships. We learn life is more fulfilling and fruitful when we distribute our blessings and share our hardships.

We are asking you, the reader, to trust us. In one sense, we are strangers—hardly someone you would trust without reservations. We encourage you to take your reservations with you. Question what we say and wonder whether we are to be trusted to help you learn how to improve your capacity and ability to forgive and be reconciled with those who have done you wrong. What has been done cannot be undone. But, what you do with what is left undone in your mind and heart can be released, reviewed, understood, and acted upon.

Although pardon may not be the solution, the act of engaging in a process wherein pardon may be the outcome can be healthy, even illuminating and exhilarating. We hope you will begin by believing that no one is beyond pardon, no one is beyond being accepted as a member of the human family. What has happened to you cannot be undone, but there is no point in giving your lifetime over to collecting punishment as a form of retribution. Sometimes the debt needs to be forgiven. Sometimes reconciliation will require a radical transformation in our attitude and a declaration of independence from the price we are exacting before we can let go. The beyond is really not as far as you might think. That place is where you will enjoy the happiness we were created to feel and the peace of a promise we long to experience. Forgiveness need not be an elusive goal or an impossible change of heart. Trust yourself to believe this axiom of the book. Trust us to take you beyond where you are and to the place where you would like to be.

Introduction

How to Think About Living: Context

TURBULENCE—ONE WORD THAT might characterize the world we live in. Not just the world about us, but the world within us. We are so busy, we almost bump into ourselves coming and going; we practically trip over ourselves and have a difficult time maintaining our balance. We know a balanced life is worth living, but how do we achieve that balance? Self-help books purport to teach us how to achieve some kind of mental, emotional, or spiritual security and stability in our lives. These books tend to emphasize the way we make decisions about our use of time. The well-balanced life is purported to be one where we use time rather than time using us. We are urged to use time on our terms and according to our priorities. And now we (your authors) come along and ask you to make the contents of <u>this</u> book and the work we are going to ask you to do a priority in your life.

Turbulence—a word that might express a restlessness and unsettled experience of living. We know the feeling but cannot put our finger on the place. We know things are not quite right, but we don't really know what is wrong. We sense life could be a lot better, but we aren't sure what would make it so. In this book, we would like you to consider disordered and disturbing relationships as a possible and plausible explanation for your disoriented view of life and your disquieting experience of living.

Turbulence—a word that might put us in touch with the tumult of an ongoing relationship or the havoc of a broken one. Relationships can be chaotic and chaos does not lend itself to making wise and prudent decisions. Rather, we are likely to let our feelings get the best of us, and unfortunately, our feelings often reveal the worst of us. In fact, we may make things worse thinking we cannot possibly permit ourselves wide latitude about what we say and do. Then the damage is done before we can collect our thoughts and weigh our alternatives. We have opened the door to a chaotic situation where one party passes through the door before a tempered course of action can be introduced.

Yet turbulence has a positive side. We want to calm the waters and smooth the sea but we cannot easily navigate in a storm of claims and counterclaims. It's all too easy to stray off course if we do nothing to correct the situation. Still we generally do not want to hastily depart or gradually drift away from people because of an angry outburst or a violent action. We want to make things right, to feel right, to do what is right. Some form of forgiveness (redirected thinking, feeling, and action) will at least momentarily appease the storm and settle the sea.

In this book we believe we can help you reduce some of the turbulence in your life. Maybe "turbulence" overstates the intensity and enormity of the conflicts that deflate your happiness and flatten your fervor for living. Nonetheless, everyone who lives and learns will encounter times when they are not all they could and can be. What we might have done to raise an awareness and make a point may not do anything to help the situation. Someone will likely take offense, and the offense will not go unnoticed.

This book does not address the ways you might behave to avoid the differences between what did happen and what should happen. It will deal with what did happen and what can be done about it. We have two active solutions—forgiveness and reconciliation. We offer one proactive solution: becoming a new creation through virtuous living. The table of contents gives a brief overview of what we have done with this book. Right now we are going to talk about what we have been thinking.

How to Think About This Book: Content

The title of this book is somewhat misleading. Although it is indeed about forgiveness and reconciliation, it is about so much more. We are intent upon getting you to make a point of being good to yourself. All goodness begins with you, the person you are, and the choices you make. Without <u>you</u> there would be no point in writing this book.

We want to use your initial interest and good intentions to re-introduce you to yourself and to welcome you back to that part of yourself lost in the daily ordinariness of living. We want to rescue you from time and energy spent on things that hardly matter and certainly do not count in the larger scheme of life. Those things are often the aftermath of disagreement and dissension and are the forerunners of discouragement, disillusionment, and defeat. They suck the very life out of you and leave you tired, drained of energy and enthusiasm. You lack some of the vitality that once sparked your desire and fueled your determination to live your dreams.

Yes, we know you are busy. Your calendar is filled with appointments, days and weeks scheduled ahead are packed with engagements. You're trying to make time to plan a vacation. You want to set aside time to start or finish a project. Unforeseen requests, emergencies, and numerous time-consuming distractions take over. You barely have enough time to get a decent night's rest much less have time for yourself. Yet, that is exactly what we are going to ask you to do. We want you to believe and behave as though you are important enough to take time for yourself. We think you can spare the time if you make up your mind to do so.

We want you to put <u>yourself</u> on your calendar. We want you to make friends with yourself. We want you to take time to decide where you are in your life, if you are where you want to be, and where you think you are going. Forgiveness and reconciliation can be used as instruments for putting yourself in touch with all of your life. They are life-lines that connect you with everything that is life-giving and life-affirming.

Since you already think of time as a commodity—taking time, spending time, using time, time to spare, time to think, time to waste—you might just as well buy some time for yourself. While we won't try to estimate the purchase price, we do know the price you pay will be well worth it. You will begin to have time and use time to participate in the primary thrust of this book – forgiveness and reconciliation – as instruments for getting into life and out of life what you want.

Your authors are reminded of a time years ago (this will certainly date us), when some hours during the day and night had no programming on television. Shortly before the television stations resumed broadcasting, they ran a test pattern that usually identified the station's call letters. This test pattern was the station's opportunity to test the strength and quality of its signal, and adjust their transmission. Then when they began to broadcast, they would be sure their viewers received a good picture.

We are using this foreword and back cover to send out a test pattern and signal. We hope the signal will be strong enough to reach you. If you are reading this foreword, we know we have successfully sent out a strong signal. Now we plan to adjust the signal for clarity. We want the image, and later the message, to be sufficiently appealing that you stay tuned. We've had to rely upon words to create our picture and convey our message. But, we don't apologize for a lack of pictures in the book because words are a powerful inducement to learn and grow.

This book is essentially about growth. As we indicate on the back cover, it is growth toward the person you can and would like to be. This is an ambitious undertaking. It involves a missionary attitude and a visionary spirit. Missionary in the sense of being sent out to be of service. In this instance, you will be in service to yourself because you cannot be for others what you cannot be for yourself. Visionary in the sense of being able to imagine your possibilities and envision a future where you are liberated from the conditions in your life and ill-chosen behaviors that currently diminish you and the quality of your life. Forgiveness and reconciliation are two of the conditions that are potentially life-giving and life-affirming. They enlist bedrock attitudes and activities in a life worth living.

We will devote one entire chapter to the virtues which serve to illuminate the need for and animate the expression of forgiveness and reconciliation. Virtues can stand on their own, but forgiveness and reconciliation cannot. They must be fed, nourished, and sustained by virtue. They depend upon virtue to forge a vision of what can be, to form the initiative to move out and fashion the commitment to remain faithful to the end. Exercising our virtues puts us in right relationship with life and enables us to humbly exalt and celebrate what it means to be human and humane.

We rely upon the disciplined work and stellar accomplishments of other people, notably the pioneering work of Robert Enright and his colleagues at the University of Wisconsin-Madison, to identify and delineate the six gateways to forgiveness. Enright and his students began the study of forgiveness in 1986, when there was hardly any psychological treatise on the topic. The Enrightian model of forgiveness is comprehensive, scientifically tested and proven. The University of Wisconsin-Madison group has worked imaginatively, diligently, resourcefully, and systematically to advance the scientific study of forgiveness in at least three areas: clear definition of forgiveness, delineating the process of forgiveness, and utilizing the process model in the context of deep and unfair hurt. Not only has their work been successfully implemented with different populations, it has advanced and popularized the study of forgiveness.

People attending conferences and participants in empirical studies often comment and appreciate the clear, concise definition of forgiveness and the lucid, easy-to-follow forgiveness process. There has been a convergence of agreement that the Enrightian how-to-forgive process appeals because of its simplicity and honesty. Honest because it makes no false claims or exaggerated promises, such as "you can forgive anything and anybody overnight." Participants like the idea that forgiveness is described as a slow, gradual process that can be followed independently, the choice is not imposed nor needs to be managed.

The six gateways that are the inner core of this book will have wide appeal for individuals who are directing their own personal growth and for helping professionals who facilitate the growth process for others. In this instance, we have in mind social workers, counselors, psychologists, pastors, and spiritual directors who want to further the healing process by attending to people suffering the debilitating effects of un-forgiveness and who are searching for the growth enhancing benefits of reconciliation and a virtue-directed life-style.

In an ancient and tragic story about a bug in a rug, the bug had to eke out his living in a beautiful Persian rug. Each day was a struggle as he made his way through the tightly knit strands and tufts of wool to find something to eat. He relied upon the gifts of food dropped from the guests who attended receptions in this room. He fussed and fumed about his dreadful situation. Complaining was about the only outlet for his frustration. His survival depended on a daily regimen of arduous work.

The tragedy of the story is that the bug lived and died in this magnificent Persian rug without ever realizing the beauty of his surroundings. Had he been able to get above the rug and view his situation from there, he would have noticed two things. First, there was a pattern in the world in which he lived. Second, those things he called his problems were part of the pattern.

You also live in a magnificent world with imaginable and exciting possibilities. But at times you get mired in the complexities and frustrations of living. Sometimes it is tough just to get through the day. You cannot see over your problems. You cannot see the larger picture.

This book will help you get "above the rug." We will point out the patterns, describe the terrain, the hills, valleys, and plains, give you a map, provide directions, and help you at various rest points along the way. This book, in some ways, will be aimed at teaching geography—the lay of the land that stretches from your heart to your mind, and vice-versa. We will invite you to be companions on a journey. Like travel agents, we have already plotted the course and taken it ourselves. We found it challenging, captivating, and enlightening. We think you will, too. We will not mislead, much less misdirect, you. The title is only a shortcut to telling you where we are going. We're not planning any shortcuts, so pack your bags and plan to stay awhile.

How to Use This Book: Method
Before you Begin
Identify one person with whom you have a rather prolonged single or multiple incidents and/or frequently occurring forgiveness issue(s) or problem(s). Record the name of this person here.

Briefly describe the significant injury, offense, or hurt (which you regard as unfair, deep, and undeserved) and continues to be a source of pain and estrangement.

Description of the affliction conditions, that is, the wrongdoing which precipitated the forgiveness crisis.

The following list you make can include responses that have actually been expressed or talked about but ones that you feel have not been sufficiently resolved; ones where forgiveness continues to be an issue.

1. List/describe the <u>feelings</u> that were expressed at the outset and continue to be problematic but are nonetheless the cause of some distress.
2. List/describe the <u>thoughts</u> that you harbor then and now.
3. List/describe the injurious <u>behavior(s)</u> you found particularly objectionable then and struggle to deal with now.

Description of action conditions.

1. List/describe some of the ways you have tried to deal with what happened?
2. List/describe your attitude about your role in resolving this problem.
3. List/describe the reasons you want to deal with the unresolved aspects of this relationship problem.

Description of intra- and inter-personal efforts to deal with the injury.

1. List/describe what you have done (direct and/or indirect) to minimize the recurrence of the hurtful behavior and/or increase the incidence of appropriate behavior.
2. List/describe the reasons you believe the relationship is getting better, is on-hold, or is getting worse despite what you or the other person has done in the form of pardoning or reconciliation.

3. List/describe the feelings that indicate the relationship is getting better, is on-hold, or is getting worse and the basis for your feeling this way.
4. Finally, using a scale of one to ten, one being poor and ten being excellent, define your current relationship with the person you identified at the outset of this exercise. That is, to what extent do the following forerunners of forgiveness define your relationship with one another?

Honesty
1 _____ 10

Patience
1 _____ 10

Compassion
1 _____ 10

Temperance
1 _____ 10

Gentleness
1 _____ 10

Trust
1 _____ 10

Understanding
1 _____ 10

Empathy
1 _____ 10

Others
1 _____ 10

CHAPTER ONE

Our Origins

Making Contact: Getting in touch with what we bring and how we use ourselves as instruments of growth.

Babies are born without kneecaps. They don't appear until the child reaches 2 to 6 years of age. It's impossible to sneeze with your eyes open.

Our eyes are always the same size from birth, but our nose and ears never stop growing. Women blink nearly twice as often as men.

Your stomach has to produce a new layer of mucus every two weeks; otherwise, it will digest itself.

Comment:

We are an absolutely fascinating species. There is so much to know about how we are constructed-physically, emotionally, intellectually, psychologically, and spiritually. The complexities can confound us. Yet there is also an underlying cell simplicity that absorbs and astounds us. We will forever be a mystery.

We are also unrelentingly curious about what and who we are. We want to know our uniqueness at the many levels of complexity. We also want to simply understand how we are all cut from the same cloth and sewn together with the common threads of our humanity.

We come first to understand forgiveness as occurring in the context of our common and uncommon ways of construing and constructing our world. We are influenced by similar potentials, hereditary and cultural; we are also shaped by the choices we make. Our success depends upon awareness, discernment, and action. We will never see and know everything we need to succeed. Nor will we ever be sufficient to put it all together and act without making mistakes.

Forgiveness is often about undoing the repercussions of our mistakes and then avoiding the repetitive perceptions and practices that were our downfall. Forgiveness is frequently the first step to heal divisions that undermine collaboration and cooperation so vital to remarkable results and enduring satisfaction.

At birth we are vulnerable and are unable to fend for ourselves. We depend upon the love and good will of others for our survival. Fortunately, we are born with all the equipment to let people know what we need. However, the way we express our needs must be understood and regarded as an acceptable demand upon others.

Vulnerability and dependency are two facets of the human condition. Much of our behavior originates in our desire to protect ourselves from the former and to release ourselves from the latter. We work at becoming and being our own person in the interest of making a place for ourselves in the world. But before we can be our own person we must learn to negotiate in a world that can be hostile and unforgiving.

Early in our lives we all feel physically vulnerable in that sometimes-hostile world. We may initially experience the feeling as discomfort and express it by crying. We must depend upon someone to interpret our experience and minister to our needs. That someone may decide we are hungry and feed us; or we have a wet or dirty diaper, and change it. Generally, we are content if one or both of these conditions are corrected.

From the beginning, we also need a certain amount of nourishment to sustain us. However, we are not capable of getting it on our own. Whoever provides our sustenance must be a willing provider. Sometimes this person does it on our schedule, sometimes not. We may feel satisfied with what we get, but when we don't, we have only one way of letting someone know about it. Sometimes, rather than being fed, we may be burped, and put back to bed, and patted gently as we lay in bed. Or we may be rocked until we go to sleep. While this wasn't what we needed, we learn to be comforted without being fed. Being comforted becomes a way of feeling fed. Learning to substitute attention and affection for food or to associate the two may later define a dimension of our personality. This originally simple and increasingly complex interchange between another and us is initially aimed at survival and eventually is aimed at personal fulfillment.

Abraham Maslow, (Toward a Psychology of Being) a psychologist who devoted much of his life to studying the antecedents of behavior, described the growth toward maturity as a process of need fulfillment. He asserted that all of our behavior is based on our efforts to satisfy one or more of six basic needs, which become motives that drive our behavior. They originate from changes in our internal world and, generally, make demands for satisfaction upon the external world. We experience them as tension or discomfort. We try to figure out what is bothering us. We select and engage in behaviors to replace negative feelings of tension with positive feelings of pleasure or satisfaction. We do not want to be without, so we choose behaviors to satisfy the longing for something more. We act our way into becoming the persons we are.

As time passes, this striving to assert our independence is bound to create conflicts with similar efforts of others. While the ends we seek are similarly felt by others, our motives and methods for getting our way may be quite different and can create tension in our relationships with others. These tensions sometimes result in offensive remarks and actions. Both parties may feel assaulted by unacceptable claims on their time, property, or person. Each may seek some form of retribution. There may be irreconcilable differences. The cross-currents of discord and disharmony bid for a solution. Forgiveness may be the solution or the impetus for trying to work things out. The success of the process will depend upon each person facing his/her vulnerability and then facing one another with a common aim to be less so.

Need Satisfaction

We always choose to do what we believe will best satisfy our needs at the time. This depends to a large extent upon how accurately we interpret our needs, the behavior we select to express our needs, the availability of choice-appropriate objects in the environment, and our proficiency in acquiring them. For example, we may experience negative feelings of physical hunger, review our mental menu of need satisfying possibilities, decide to seek satisfaction at our favorite drive-in, match our mental menu with their offerings, purchase the item, and find pleasure in our sense of taste. The same discomfort or need may produce a very different menu and sequence of actions at another time.

The complexities associated with this single need depend upon a multitude of factors, both genetic and environmental.

Physical Needs

Our physical needs are not confined to hunger. We also thirst. As we will learn later, this physical desire to quench a need for fluid may also be expressed as a psychological "thirst for knowledge."

We also seek pleasure in physically sensual experiences. Our skin is the most sensitive of all our organs and covers our entire body. We are sensitive to many forms of touch and can express a wide range of feelings through touching behaviors. Touch accompanied by the sight and sounds of another accentuate the experience. It's little wonder that a meal taken in the company of a loved one can be a complete sensual experience, fulfilling on a physical level.

Maslow characterized physical needs as the most potent of all our needs; our survival depends upon satisfying our physical need. After having been fed, and being reasonably free of the tension associated with this need, another less potent need emerges. We reach to achieve a similar level of satisfaction with our need for safety to survive.

Safety Needs

We need protection from the elements and from one another. Climate and geography will greatly influence the choices we make and the availability of choice-related materials. However, competition for food and material resources may contribute to adversarial relationships. Protection against others complicates our satisfaction for safety needs. People can be troublesome, competitive, violent, and destructive. These security and safety issues may create tension, make us feel intimidated, and create a need to protect ourselves from potentially life-threatening experiences. Fear of losing one's job, the means to food and shelter, is another experience that contributes to behaviors to insure continued employment and a safe and secure future. The comfort of a physically safe and secure environment, free of threat to one's person and livelihood, are sought as minimum requirements for a fruitful life.

Psychological Needs

We have a need to be loved, to belong, and to feel good about ourselves. It is not enough to survive in a physical sense; psychological survival is also necessary. People will even choose to deprive themselves of some physical comforts associated with food and safety in order to feel they belong one with others. For as infants, early survival depends upon someone loving them and belonging to them. As infants, a baby needs parents because he/she couldn't survive without them. They love the child because he/she appealed to their reciprocal need for food and safety.

In this way we are connected to one another in the vulnerabilities of our human condition, using our mutual dependencies to identify with one another. As time goes on, infants offer parents small tokens of their appreciation- cooing, gurgling, and smiling to keep each engaged with the other. At first a marriage of convenience, these psychological needs become a covenant of mutual caring and understanding.

Esteem Needs

Our self-esteem, thinking well of ourselves, depends upon our ability to give and to receive and upon a similar receptiveness and capability in others. We embrace one another in our longing to be loved and in our desire to be somebody. We reinforce our connection to others by returning their love and including them in our circle of important people.

Deficiency Needs

Maslow designated these four needs: physical, safety, love and belonging, and esteem, as deficiency, or dependency needs. The term "deficiency" is used to express the absence of sufficient need satisfaction; we may create tension and feelings of inadequacy through these dependency needs. Dependency describes the idea that satisfaction of these needs depends upon external circumstances gradually brought under our control.

As we grow up, the distinction between physical and psychological needs becomes blurred. For example, we can hunger for love and belonging, but we may "eat" too little or too much in our effort to find a need fulfilling experience in this area. We may not feel safe in our relations with others. We may find some people threatening. Even though they do not jeopardize our need for a safe physical environment, they may make us feel anxious and fearful because we cannot live up to their expectations. We may seek protection from these feelings by becoming excessively dependent upon them for attention and approval. Or we may avoid them because they rouse unsettling feelings.

Forgiveness in the Context of Need Satisfaction

It may be more difficult to forgive someone who has been an impediment to satisfying a deficiency need. Because these needs grow stronger when denied, any infringement of them will be experienced as more intense emotions, variants of anger (bitterness or resentment), or variants of fear (dread or timidity). These strong active and passive emotions can evoke serious relationship problems. Since behavior choices are often intended to achieve self-sufficiency and self-aggrandizement, need satisfaction is often fraught with conflict while begging for understanding. Forgiveness will, of necessity, become a party to transactions grounded in this combination of motives and choices.

It's not surprising that Maslow refers to these deficiency needs as being prepotent, we become preoccupied with satisfying these needs. They dominate our feelings and create tensions. The need is more potent to satisfy one need below the next higher needs. Hunger is more potent than safety, safety more potent than love and belonging, love and belonging more potent than self-esteem. While we would normally seek some degree of need-satisfaction at one level before being motivated to seek satisfaction at the next, if we have to spend most of our time satisfying physical and safety needs, we have little energy to invest in building relationships that satisfy belonging and esteem needs. However, in the interest of satisfying higher level needs, some people deny themselves the satisfaction of lower level needs.

Many relationships in our early history as a species were devoted almost exclusively to cooperation for survival. Our ancestors were preoccupied with getting their next meal and seeking shelter from dangerous animals and unpredictable nature. Today, affluence and freedom from elementary survival needs have enabled us to devote more of our time, attention, and energy to forming and building relationships. Magazines, books, and movies attest to our desire to understand and cultivate human relationships. Despite our good intentions, we are often imperfect when it comes to relationship-oriented need satisfaction. Family breakdowns, domestic violence, incest, and a multitude of other relationship problems reveal our inability to find adequate expression and appropriate satisfaction for these interpersonal (love and belonging) and intrapersonal (esteem) psychological needs.

Deficiency needs grow stronger when denied. When a lack of forgiveness is associated with any one of these needs, the concomitant feelings of tension also grow stronger. One source of tension might be attributed to the residual effects of conflict. You might have gotten what you wanted but at an unacceptable cost or expense. For instance, one person consenting to eat at the restaurant of another's choice may produce a disagreement. Both parties may feel some ill will toward the other and neither has a totally satisfying outing. Conciliatory conversation may be started to restore a favorable balance in the relationship. Another example is meeting a couple's future security needs at the expense of doing things and having material goods now. If the parties cannot agree on similar financial viewpoints, capitulation by one may be accompanied by growing resentment. Some form of compromise may be needed in the interest of restoring harmony. Without forgiveness, the feelings that precipitated the compromise might result in a less than satisfying resolution of the problem. Since our actions generally have consequences for others, often unforeseen and unpleasant, forgiveness is an ongoing feature of living.

Growth Needs

The growth needs of knowledge and understanding, aesthetic expression, and self-actualization follow these deficiency needs. Maslow characterized them as growth and autonomy seeking needs. When free of the conforming constraints associated with depending, we can invest more energy in the satisfaction of inner-inspired motives. These motives spring more from an individual's unique genetic and experiential history. The time and energy garnered from the ease of satisfying other motives allows us to pursue personal interests and talents. The potency of these motives becomes more acute when satisfied. The need to find an outlet for them is an outgrowth of the "taken-for-granted" status of lower level needs.

As we noted earlier, tension mounts when needs go unfulfilled. Deficiency needs grow strong when denied, whereas growth needs grow stronger when satisfied. Thus we have an insatiable curiosity to know and understand. Sometimes the search is directed toward achieving a better grasp of our situation in life, the people we know, or the ends we seek. Often, we search for beauty and grace in all its forms. We strive to rise above the obvious and ordinariness of life. We are no longer merely content to simply satisfy our lower level needs. We learn to embellish upon them. We occasionally want to dine in elegance. We confer with architects to design our dwellings. Needs become elevated to wants. We can get by with less, but we are not willing to accept less. Wants also create tension and seek release through want-satisfying experiences.

Whether wants or needs, our lives are managed or regulated in the service of these ends. Even at rest, our dreams work on unresolved issues or prepare us for the unforeseen. We never stop needing or wanting. Only as we bring down the curtain on one need or combination thereof does another take center stage.

Where does forgiveness fit into the picture? Because affluence has given us a gift of time, we worry less about making a living and more about having a life. We want more from life than enough to eat and a place to stay. We want to feel important and be important. Other people who matter and are important to us are essential in satisfying these feelings. Thus, we form relationships as an outgrowth of mutual need-satisfying experiences, which help define and express our very essence.

Relationships are two-way need exchanging experiences. However, the give and take is often not an even exchange. Tension mounts when the unevenness persists over a long period of time. Resentment sometimes builds, as one party feels exploited. Unkind words or perilous actions might be exchanged. Both parties feel the tension and want this situation to be over and done with. However, they can't bring themselves to a resolution. So they may press into service other needs, hoping to substitute need-fulfillment in these areas for a lack of satisfying relationship experiences. But the energy to suppress relationship needs in the interest of elevating lower level needs takes its toll. Fatigue can be an ever-present reminder of their problem. Striving to keep hostility in check, or holding off saying "I'm sorry" is an emotional drain on some people's psyche.

Forgiveness as a Need

Like a need, lacking or withholding forgiveness can be a prepotent factor in your life. You may become preoccupied with the situation that provoked the tension and this can become a constant reminder of something negative, or possibly divisive. Like being hungry or thirsty, you cannot get your mind off of it. As you go about satisfying other needs, lurking in the background is the tension-producing need to re-establish a meaningful relationship. Nothing else is fully satisfying because this aspect of a fully functioning self is absent. Competing for the foremost attention, forgiveness can become a prepotent motive. Without taking a step toward forgiveness, the rest of life leaves you feeling dissatisfied and unfulfilled.

At a very basic level we can hunger for forgiveness. We can breathe more easily when this burden is lifted from our shoulders. Comforted by knowing we have released someone from the burden or have been released ourselves; we can look down the road and face the future with an improved sense of well-being. We feel renewed and revitalized. When the prepotent need to be fed by forgiveness is satisfied, we might seek to restore the secure feeling of being able to count on another. Even though we know risks are involved, that trusting is vulnerability we choose. We can venture forth from the safety of relying upon ourselves. We take a chance on life because the prospects seem worth going beyond sheer survival needs.

Despite our best efforts to manage need-satisfaction, we are bound to be hurt and disappointed from time to time. Forgiveness for our own shortcomings and others is an ever-present reminder that "safe and secure" are relative conditions. We are constantly revising what we expect and what we will settle for. We often have to bridge the difference by forgiving ourselves and/or others.

Synthesis

Relationship building is a natural outgrowth of our efforts to more fully satisfy physical and safety needs. We cannot long endure the loss of meaningful human relationships. We depend upon one another for physical survival and emotional survival. The same emotions that drive the need for belonging and self-esteem also drive the need for forgiveness. Belonging is worked out daily in the imperfect transactions between and among people. The imperfections may be due to hungering too much or protecting too little. Both vulnerabilities contribute to ill-advised goals and inappropriate behavior choices, causing conflicts that produce tension. The release from this tension often requires a resolution grounded in interpersonal relationships. Forgiveness is an integral element that sustains the process and ultimately contributes to love and intimacy.

Our relationships occur along a continuum as we refer to some people as strangers, others as acquaintances, and some few as friends. All of these relationships occur within the larger context of the human family. Forgiving, or the lack of it, affects individual relationships as well as the well-being of this larger community. Whether relationships occur by chance or by choice we share a common destiny. Common decency and a civility grounded in respect and reciprocity bear us up in hard times. Joyful inclusion, knowing and sharing our most noble aspirations celebrate the best of times. The relationship is not merely a marriage of convenience; rather, it is a covenant worthy of our faithfulness.

On a personal level, vital and vigorous relationships are the key to our survival. Our emotional lives and our mental health depend upon finding ways to cooperate with others and to free us from the emotional turmoil of unresolved conflicts with our contemporaries. Without some form of stable relationships, we are constantly putting out conflict fires. We have to put some things behind us, and forgiveness is often the best choice. While forgiving is not necessarily forgetting, it is at least setting aside in the interest of going on. Getting on with life, in a Maslow expressed hierarchy, permits us to devote some of ourselves to growth needs.

Life is about growth, and this book is about growth. The search to find purpose and meaning in life is a journey that we all undertake. Our paths will lead us to a chosen destination, but we must be perceptive and persistent. This book is intended to serve both purposes. We think it has great utility because it addresses what matters to people who want more from life than what they are getting or giving.

Each chapter produces a gateway to growth with guideposts along the route. As you proceed along the gateways we will challenge your thinking, feelings, and actions. We will ask you to consider these three aspects of behavior as separate and distinct entities as we investigate their contributions to a total behavior. We will draw you into the joint interaction and integration of these behaviors. The aim is to help you think, feel, and act as a whole. The proper alignment of these elements of behavior will enable you to believe with conviction, value with patient endurance, and act with integrity.

The process of bringing ourselves to completeness is never over until we are denied additional opportunities. This book is directed to the in-between time, to right now when the possibilities are unlimited. We hope this book will stretch the limits you desire and take you beyond what you thought possible.

Footnote

In the first frame of a 3-panel <u>Peanuts</u> cartoon, Charlie Brown says to Linus, "My grandpa says those were the good days." Linus responds, "What days?" Charlie Brown concludes, "He doesn't know what days, but he is sure those were the good days."

Comment:

We often think the good days are somewhere in the past where we cannot recover them, and maybe not even rediscover them. Actually, the good days are still ahead of us. We are born needy and we will not be content to put all of our eggs in one basket.

CHAPTER TWO

Forgiving is Unnatural

Making Contact: Our Assumption—Forgiving is Unnatural.

YEARS AGO A memorable song from *Annie Get Your Gun* included a line, "doing what comes naturally." Generally we feel more comfortable doing what comes naturally. It does depend some on how natural.

Story:

Two priests decided to go to Hawaii on vacation. They were determined to make this a "real" vacation by not wearing anything that would identify them as clergy.

As soon as the plane landed, they headed for a store and bought some really outrageous shorts, shirts, sandals, and sunglasses. The next morning they went to the beach dressed in their "tourist" garb.

They were sitting on the beach chairs enjoying a drink, the sunshine, and the scenery when a "drop dead gorgeous" blonde in a tiny bikini came walking straight toward them. As the blonde passed, she smiled and said, "Good morning, Father" to each of them. Both were stunned. How in the world did she know they were priests?

Next day, they went back to the store and bought even more outrageous outfits. Once again they settled on their chairs to enjoy the sunshine. The same gorgeous blonde, wearing a string bikini this time came walking towards them. Again, as she approached, she greeted them individually: "Good Morning, Father."

One of the priests couldn't stand it and said, "Just a minute young lady."

"Yes," she replied.

"We are priests and proud of it, but I have to know, how in the world did you know we were priests?"

The blonde replied, "Father, it's me, Sister Mary Angela!"

Comment:

However, there are times we prefer to diverge from what comes naturally. We want to experience an out of the ordinary side of life. We want to step outside and aside from the boundaries that frame our lives. We picture ourselves living another reality. Occasionally the new reality exposes us to something novel and unanticipated. We see with a new set of eyes. We may be surprised by what we failed to recognize before.

The confluence of circumstances may put us in an unexpected place with an unpredictable consequence. Forgiveness can be like that, too. We dress down or dress up so we feel different about our place and position in the world. In this new role we try on another side of life. We may take a vacation from our accustomed ways of representing ourselves to others. We let down our guard long enough to let our imagination work overtime. We may be surprised to see what we have been missing by being so entrenched in a "single" way of living. The unnatural can be quite revealing, naturally.

This chapter begins with our basic assumption about forgiveness, a theme that carries throughout the chapter. Next, we support this assumption by enumerating several major roadblocks to forgiving. We'll describe these and then give a rebuttal to them. Finally, we'll focus on a fourth roadblock, which consists of a number of misconceptions that are described and rebutted. Let's begin with our assumption.

Our Basic Assumption: Forgiving is Unnatural

The central assumption of this book is that forgiving is unnatural. The reasons will be discussed after first clarifying what we mean by "unnatural."

Forgiving is unnatural in the sense that we are not automatically inclined to forego our right to punish the person who injured us. The spontaneous reaction to having been hurt by someone emotionally, psychologically, morally, or physically is far from compassionate. Our immediate response is usually to get back at that person.

By maintaining that forgiving is unnatural we do not mean that it is impossible for humans to forgive each other. It is indeed within the human capacity to forgive, but the act of forgiving takes time and is painful. Paradoxically, the pain we suffer while trying to forgive the other is a pain that frees us from the initial hurt. Pain can be transformed into a positive force that empowers, energizes, and liberates us. Through forgiving, it is possible for humans to conquer the host of negative emotions that they experience when they are injured deeply and unfairly.

How to forgive is discussed in the next chapters. The remainder of this chapter examines a number of roadblocks that make forgiving difficult and unnatural.

Roadblock 1: Negative Feelings

A number of factors coalesce to make forgiving unnatural. To begin with, when someone deeply and unfairly hurts us, we experience many negative feelings such as anger, resentment, shame, rage, and even hatred. We invariably believe that these feelings *happen* to us, and we unconsciously become unwilling to admit that we can control our feelings. We reason that since feelings happen to us, we just cannot help feeling the way we do. In other words, we allow ourselves to react to feelings in a victimized, out-of-control manner.

People who feel powerless and helpless would not find it in their hearts to forgive. In this sense, forgiving is unnatural because it enables the victimized person to reverse the tide of powerlessness. It supplies the individual with a new way of looking at feelings—that feelings can eventually be brought under control. Strong emotions can be tamed if the individual actively, willingly, consciously, and willfully engages in the unnatural process of bringing them under control. This must be done without denying that the feelings do exist and do affect us emotionally and physically.

When a friend betrays a deep secret of ours, we feel disappointed, hurt, and betrayed. This is natural. What is unnatural at the moment we find out that we have been betrayed is to remain levelheaded, calm, and continue to deal with that friend in a compassionate, trusting, and respectful manner. This would be impossible initially and would make forgiving our friend an almost impossible option. It would be easier and more natural to get back at or ignore our friend. But the hurt goes on, and the shock, disbelief, and disappointment that our friend did that to us is rehearsed in our minds and hearts. This perpetuates the hurt and creates a vicious, victimized cycle that takes its toll on us. As time passes, we might discover that how we have been feeling was largely of our own choosing and therefore we must decide to change the way we feel to get better. If we do, we begin to engage in one of the unnatural steps of forgiving the other.

Believing that we do not control our feelings is only one dimension of the unnaturalness of forgiving. Roadblock 2—another equally important aspect of this unnatural process is our urge to retaliate.

Roadblock 2: Tendency to Retaliate

When someone hurts us profoundly and undeservedly, we feel an injustice was dealt to us. A state of internal imbalance exists, and we must set the scale of justice aright. We begin to seek retribution by inflicting pain equal to or more than what we received. Our natural disposition is an attack posture—to mete out punishment and act on our resentment or rage. The unnatural course is to immediately take the path of liberation and healing when a person deals us an unfair blow. Consider the following example:

> When John was growing up, he did not like his father. His father criticized him constantly and called him degrading names frequently. In return, John thought of ways to get back at his father. This animosity turned into revengeful thoughts that resulted in a behavior that infuriated his dad. Although not an early riser, John would creep out of his bed in the morning, sneak into the garage, and deflate all

four tires on his father's vehicle. This made his dad extremely upset and caused him to be late for work many times. John confessed that the more he did it, the more satisfied he was. Revenge, like a drug, became addicting.

Just when his dad did not suspect that someone might deflate his car tires, John would do it again. He wanted his dad to be fired from his job so he would experience some of the feelings of worthlessness that John had. It was not until some time later that John realized his revenge seeking was getting out of hand, and that he probably would never be able to even the score with his dad.

When John was 20, he realized that he could not cling on to the past and react to his dad's negative behaviors. He had a lot to work through before he abdicated to the course of mercy and forgave his dad.

If we do indeed get over our urge to retaliate, we might then become entrapped by our feelings of pride.

Roadblock 3: Pride

Our pride gets wounded when someone transgresses against us. Pride can blind us to the fact that forgiving is an act of courage, not weakness. But it is not natural to feel okay within ourselves when someone offends our sense of dignity. The natural response is to preserve our dignity by assuming a posture of pride, by thinking more about ourselves, and less about the person who injured us. Pride makes us look down upon the person who offended us. It makes us believe that we are better. The following story illustrates the blinding power of pride.

Mary was a faithful wife to her husband, Mike, and a loving mother to their two sons. Her husband was kind and gentle when he was sober, but verbally and physically abusive to her and the children when drunk, which was at least once a week. Refusing to admit his alcohol problem, Mike rejected his family's pleas to seek professional help. Mary and her children could not take the frequent abuse any longer. She filed for divorce. Following the divorce, Mary entered counseling to relieve her feelings of depression and anger. Mary told the counselor she would never forgive her husband for the irreparable damage he did to her and the children throughout their 12 years of marriage.

Even after nine months in counseling, Mary felt that Mike was a despicable individual. She often said, "Why couldn't Mike have been more like me? Why didn't he respect and care for our family as I did? Why did he have to be so selfish, choosing alcohol over me and his family?" Mary's relatives and friends reinforced these feelings. They told her how great she was and how low and base Mike was.

Mary's feelings about Mike didn't change even when she learned that Mike had been receiving counseling and was making remarkable progress in his recovery from alcoholism. Mike's apologies, verbal and written, offered no change in Mary's negative attitude toward him. She believed Mike could never undo the harm he had done nor begin to fulfill her expectations. Mike was not worthy of forgiveness much less respect.

Mary's depression and anger got worse. Her children reminded her of Mike, the abuser. She began to take out her frustration on them.

When an individual's sense of pride is injured, it is natural for that person to protect him/herself. However, what begins as a natural self-protection mechanism may turn into self-righteousness. As in Mary's case, she could not separate Mike as a person from his alcoholism. She would not allow herself to see Mike's redeeming qualities because she was obsessed with his drinking. She saw Mike as someone who would never measure up, who was not worthy of her respect, and who would consequently remain unloved.

Assuming forgiveness was out of the question. It would be unnatural for Mary to adopt a posture of love and compassion in the face of her husband's constant abuse. Drawing upon love instead of hate, understanding instead of anger, humility instead of pride, and respect instead of debasement in response to transgressions is indeed unnatural, but not impossible. We make it possible by forging a well-balanced mixture of mind and heart. We actively seek to rid ourselves of the thoughts and feelings that make us look down upon the person who hurt us. We make a distinction between the person and what he/she did. We acknowledge that what the person did was wrong and hurtful. While we may never acknowledge our part in the problem, we can gradually think less negatively of the other, and be more reasonable with respect to their position. Surrendering our need to regain control of the situation through self-righteousness, we are free to forgive.

Having discussed the role of pride as a way of bolstering our stance against forgiving, we now move to the next section, which examines our misconceptions about forgiving and forgiveness.

Roadblock 4: Misconceptions about Forgiving

In times of personal hurt, people's misconceptions about forgiving make them naturally prone to being unforgiving.

Misconception #1: Fear of having our good intentions misunderstood.
This common misconception makes us apprehensive of how the other person might construe our good intentions. The injurer might conclude that what he/she did was okay and thereby relinquish responsibility for solving the problem. In other words, we fear that forgiving suggests we are at least partially to blame. And if we forgive, we're offering ourselves up to be hurt again and again.

Misconception #2: Fear of being viewed as weak and defenseless.
Closely related to the first misconception is the belief that the injurer and others might consider us weak or defenseless if we do not choose to retaliate or seek retribution. Friends might urge us not to "let him/her get away with it," or "let him/her off the hook."

Misconception #3; Loss of self-respect.
Sometimes provocation becomes a test of our strength. We embroil ourselves in a fight just to prove we will safeguard our self-respect. What would be unnatural is to sacrifice our desire to get even or to willingly give up our right to punish the other.

Misconception #4: Fear of reconciliation.
Some people fear that if they forgive the person who hurt them, then they must communicate their act of forgiving and be responsible for reestablishing a relationship with that individual. This fear would naturally inhibit an individual from taking the initiative to forgive the injurer, especially if the injurer continues to be belligerent.

In this case, forgiving is mistakenly equated with the act of reconciliation. Getting together with the person who has caused us pain would be the last thing on our mind and heart. Here, the following case of a battered wife illustrates this point.

> JoAnn's husband battered her constantly. To escape the severe abuse, she got up one day and left her husband. She stayed in a women's shelter for a while until she felt safe enough to venture out and start a new life. JoAnn indicated to her psychotherapist that she still loved her husband, but did not feel that it would be safe to go back to him. She knew he would start hurting her again.
>
> By equating forgiving with reconciling, JoAnn naturally opted for the safer alternative—staying away and not forgiving. While reconciliation is sometimes an unwise thing to do as in Joann's case, a person can forgive without behaviorally getting together with the other. JoAnn can forgive her husband but not reconcile with him until she feels physically and psychologically safe with him.

Misconception #5: Forgiveness will occur on its own.
Another prevalent misconception about forgiveness is that it will happen on its own, merely through the passage of time. Time is, indeed, one of the critical

factors in the act of forgiveness, but time alone does not heal all wounds. In fact, some wounds get worse with time.

We need to take an active role in the process of forgiveness by willfully and willingly confronting, working through, and resolving our pain. We also need to acknowledge that forgiving a person who has hurt us deeply will be a slow and gradual process. In some cases, such as incest and rape, the journey to healing can be extremely slow. Only small fragments of the experience can be surrendered because the pain of lifting them from one's soul can be excruciating.

If healing is left to time alone, a person's pain and suffering are likely to multiply, making the issue all the more difficult to resolve. The following case of a betrayed friend illustrates this point.

> Mary and Stephanie were long-time friends and shared many secrets. Mary told Stephanie a sensitive piece of information about Mary's relationship with her boss. Stephanie divulged this to a person on friendly terms with the boss. As a result, Mary was fired and without a job for a long time.
>
> Mary felt betrayed, disappointed, and very angry with Stephanie. She ended her friendship with Stephanie and completely wrote Stephanie out of her life. Mary thought that by ignoring Stephanie her life would gradually get back to normal again. As time passed, however, Mary became more resentful and bitter toward Stephanie. She often wished that Stephanie were dead. Mary was consumed by strong feelings of hatred and revenge and wanted to get back at Stephanie. Fortunately, Mary never carried out her vengeful plans of killing Stephanie. However, when reentering the job market, Mary was extremely cautious in selecting her friends.

Mary's case poignantly shows that the passage of time can exacerbate rather than heal deep wounds. The more pain is left undealt with, the more it grows and festers, bringing with it more undue suffering. In other words, the person becomes more victimized the longer he/she hangs on to the pain. However, time can become an asset when a person actively engages in resolving the source of pain. Forgiving another person is not a natural process that unfolds on its own. An individual has to initiate it, maintain it, and carry it through.

Misconception #6: Fear of being perceived wrongly by others.
An additional misconception about the act of forgiving deals with how the person who has hurt us and possibly other people in the community might perceive us. This misconception keeps us from choosing forgiveness as a way to resolve the pain for at least four reasons. First, we fear our act of forgiving might be interpreted as an act of weakness, submissiveness, or subordination. Second, we worry forgiveness might empower our transgressor at our own expense. Third, we are concerned about the potential social /community damage to our reputation. Fourth, we feel that without punishing the transgressor, he/she could become a perpetual perpetrator of pain.

Misconception #7: People must communicate their forgiveness to the person who wounded them.
The essence of this misconception stems from equating forgiving with reconciling. Many people believe they must communicate their forgiveness to the injurer for forgiveness to be complete. Forgiveness does make it possible for a person to reconcile with the injurer. However, as mentioned earlier, sometimes it is impossible to reconcile with the person who hurt us if that person is nowhere to be found or is not alive. Also, reconciliation may be unwise or unsafe if the perpetrator continues to hurt or is a potential source of hurt.

The compelling character of this misconception makes forgiving an out-of-the-question option. However, we must realize it is possible to forgive a person without verbally communicating it to him/her. When we forgive, we gradually release the injurer from accountability for the action. Making amends does not become the central issue in dissolving the hurt. We give up resentment and the right to punish the other. Our burden is lightened as our view of the injurer changes; we no longer see him/her as just the person who injured us. Instead, we see the person as a human being who is equal to us in humanity. For us to be able to see our injurer in this different, more accepting light requires taking an active and conscious role in the unnatural process of forgiveness.

Misconception #8: Denying will make it go away.
Sometimes we want to avoid doing anything about hurtful situations. We prefer to deny or conceal any feelings of hurt, especially when someone hurts us deeply and unfairly. Some may do this initially or sometime after the injury. This misconception is grounded in the belief that the person did not intend to hurt us, or did not actually hurt us, so there is no need to do anything. If we believe this, it is natural to act as if nothing happened, regardless of how grave the injury was. It would be unnatural to resort to forgiving in this case since we believe there is "really" nothing to forgive.

A number of explanations can be offered for people's motives for denial. To begin with, some people do not acknowledge the hurt for fear of being vulnerable, of mistakenly being perceived as weak, or of lacking self-respect. We must protect our egos at all costs—even at the unanticipated cost of our mental and perhaps physical health. Another motivating reason could simply be a natural attempt to avoid additional pain, hoping it will go away. Initially, denial provides temporary shelter from pain; we become accustomed to this protection and yearn to be sheltered even more. The unnatural act of forgiveness enables us to venture out from our shelter and meet pain head on. We discover that it is painful, but perhaps we will discover the hurt we temporarily endure will eventually and paradoxically offset the intensity of the original pain.

Misconception #9: Forgiveness is for Super Humans.
A final misconception deals with the idea that it takes a superhuman person to forgive. This is a very common misconception that the authors frequently hear from clients. Consider Janet's case:

After Janet gave birth to her first baby through C-section, her doctor tied her tubes without her consent while Janet was still under anesthesia. Her husband told her that the doctor thought if she got pregnant again, the delivery would again necessitate a C-section. This procedure could endanger her life. In shock, the husband consented to the procedure. But, the doctor never sought Janet's consent, and this made her extremely upset.

When one of the authors talked on the topic of forgiveness to a group that Janet belonged to, Janet commented, "I am convinced that forgiveness is something that saints do, not humans. How can I forgive that .... for what he did! I will never be able to get pregnant again. You say forgive that.......; I say sue him!" The presenter's response was that forgiveness could exist side by side with justice. Even if the lawsuit is brought against the doctor and is won, that still does not guarantee the feelings of anger and resentment will go away. We have to make a choice between living with the hurt, anger, and resentment, or giving that up to live more fully.

Roadblock 5: Not Knowing How to Forgive

Since forgiveness is unnatural, we must be taught directly or indirectly how to forgive. In fact, the act of forgiving is often considered socially undesirable. Forgiving is equated with being weak, nonassertive, naive, and even dangerous. In the mass media, the Rambo-like heroes are usually the ones who wreak the most havoc and whose acts of violence are glamorized.

The immediate environment we live in has a strong impact on whether we choose forgiveness attitudes and strategies in response to conflict. If our parents have modeled the use of forgiveness for us, we will more than likely look for ways to go about it. But how many individuals can attest to such modeling? To what extent does forgiveness within the family transfer to situations outside the home? What if our parents have not had anyone to model forgiving for them? Does that mean they are incapable of employing forgiveness as a means of dealing with hurt?

These answers lie in our understanding of forgiveness as a process rather than a single act. The process of pain reduction or hurt relief represents our best way of handling the situation at the time. Forgiveness may not be an option at all unless we have seen it modeled, believe in its effectiveness, and, more importantly, know how to do it. If not, we often take one of two routes—one does not involve the person who hurt us and one does. Those choosing the first path engage in activities such as physical exercise or reading that bring them relief—which is often short-lived. Others use, or even abuse, alcohol or other drugs to deal with their hurt. Needless to say, this route can be very destructive to the individual and to other relationships.

The second route a hurt person can take involves the injurer and consists of justice or mercy. Those who choose the justice path might either use legal justice to set the scale aright, or decide to mete out the punishment themselves. If the mercy route is chosen, the person may decide to forego resentment and punishment or may even choose to offer compassion.

It is possible for a person to know how to forgive but decide not to forgive. Sometimes, it is just easier to ignore the injurer and write that person out of your life. Initially, not coming to terms with your anger may be functional, but avoiding the situation as a permanent solution only exacerbates the problem. The anger lingers beneath the surface of behavior, waiting to be exposed to the light of awareness and understanding. Squarely confronting the anger, resentment, and hostility requires the mobilization of will and courage. Anything less could be irresponsible and incapacitating.

Conclusion

The goal of this chapter was to increase your understanding of the many roadblocks to forgiving. In the following chapter, you'll have an opportunity to examine the roadblocks and ask yourself if any of these are obstacles to forgiveness in your life. By doing this, you have begun to seriously consider the role of forgiveness in your life. The next chapter will also invite you to participate in the process of forgiveness. This process will help you get in touch with some aspects of unforgiveness in your life and challenge you to consider the benefits of forgiveness as a life choice.

Footnote:

There was once a little boy who had a bad temper. His father gave him a bag of nails and told him that every time he lost his temper, he should hammer a nail into the back of the fence. The first day the boy drove 37 nails into the fence.

Over the next few weeks, as he learned to control his anger, the number of nails hammered daily gradually dwindled. The boy discovered it was easier to hold his temper than to drive those nails into the fence. Finally the day came when the boy didn't lose his temper at all. He told his father about it and the father suggested that the boy now pull out one nail for each day that he was able to hold his temper.

The days passed and the young boy was finally able to tell his father that all the nails were gone. The father took his son by the hand and led him to the fence. He said, "You have done well, my son, but look at the holes in the fence. The fence will never be the same. When you say things in anger, they leave a scar just like these. You can put a knife in a man and draw it out, but it won't matter how many times you say I'm sorry—the wound is still there."

A verbal wound is as bad as a physical one. Friends are a very rare jewel, indeed. Friends are better companions than anger and a bad temper. Prize one and pity the other. They make you smile and encourage you to succeed. They lend an ear, they share words of praise, and they always want to open their hearts to us.

Comment:

Anger and bad tempers are compatible companions. It is so natural for one to precede or follow the other. Saying "I'm sorry" just doesn't always cut it. Anger and bad tempers cling together like lint on a blanket. They need to be pulled apart and separated. When you do this, you'll find it is easier to remove the behavior (bad temper) than the emotion (anger). We <u>behave</u> ourselves into the person we want to be.

CHAPTER THREE

Revenge is Natural

"**Revenge is the natural reaction to transgression.**"

Hannah Arendt

Making Contact: Technology as a safeguard

Story:
WE HAVE ALL learned to live with "voice mail" as a necessary part of modern life. But have you wondered, "What if God decided to install voice mail?" Imagine praying and hearing this:

Thank you for calling My Father's House. Please select one of the following options:

- Press 1 for Requests
- Press 2 for Thanksgiving
- Press 3 for Complaints
- Press 4 for All Other Inquiries

What if God used the familiar excuse… "I'm sorry, all of our angels are busy helping other sinners right now. However, your prayer is important to us and will be answered in the order it was received, so please stay on the line."

Comment:

You might actually prefer voice mail when dealing with the volatile emotions of revenge. The absence of someone on the other end of the line could be liberating. You remove the anxious wondering about how he/she might react to even hearing your voice and their initial response. Talking to a machine removes all the uncertainty that makes the initial encounter so frightening. Maybe knowing when you are likely to get voice mail would be a safe way to start the process. Wouldn't it be wonderful if the person responds with a voice mail thereby getting you off the hook? Your on-line voice mail instructions might sound like this:

> Press 1 if you want to talk by phone.
> Press 2 if you want to get together.
> Press 3 if you are serious about acknowledging your part in our disagreement.
> Press 4 if you believe I am to blame for our current conflict.
> Press 5 if none of the above apply.

In the previous chapter we stated that forgiveness is unnatural; in this chapter we assert that revenge, the antithesis of forgiveness, is natural. Revenge is part of our everyday life. Although malignant, revenge is a universal and pervasive human reaction. Revenge is so natural and universal because it is "an attractive, seductive, triumphant, and unusual feeling" (Barreca, 1995, p.3). Themes of revenge abound in our daily lives in cartoons, movies, novels, literature, mythology, and media. You'll find more clichés or exhortations for revenge than for forgiveness, such as: "getting even," "don't get mad, get even," "settle the score," "balance the scales of justice," "give them a taste of their own medicine," "make 'em pay!" "the dish of revenge is sweetest when cold," "revenge is sweet." In contrast, we find many fewer clichés exhorting forgiveness such as: "forgive and forget," "let bygones be bygones," and "turn the other cheek." We must, therefore, stop and think about why revenge has such a profound grip on the human psyche.

We begin by examining what revenge is and is not; what are the types of revenge; why we seek revenge; what the potential consequences of revenge are for the avenger and avenged; and what are the alternatives to revenge.

What Revenge Is

Philosophers and psychologists offer many definitions for revenge. The definitions discussed in this section are in one way or another based on the two meanings of the word "revenge" found in the Oxford English Dictionary: (1) The act of doing hurt or harm to another in return for wrong or injury suffered; satisfaction obtained by repayment of injuries; and (2) A desire to repay injuries by inflicting hurt in return. Let's look at some of the definitions of revenge.

To begin with, revenge is seen as the act of returning harm in righteous response to a perceived harm or injustice. In their work entitled The Study of Revenge in the Workplace, Bies and Tripp defined revenge as a reactive action that a wronged or harmed person takes to cause harm, damage, injury, discomfort, or punishment to the injurer or wrongdoer. The 19th century German philosopher Nietsche, defined revenge in his 1887 book Genealogy of Morals as the defensive action one takes to restore his/her honor. Nietzsche confused revenge with retribution when he argued that vengeful acts are crucial to both asserting one's sense of power and worth and for establishing a sense of justice. Revenge may also be seen as a calculated and reasoned form of non-moral resentment. Similarly, revenge is described as returning suffering to the offender for the moral evil he/she voluntarily committed (Hart, 1968). This definition is based on the assumption that return of suffering is just, or morally good. In his 1956 book, The Psychology of Interpersonal Relations, Fritz Heider viewed revenge as an act of achieving a sense of personal balance following an injury. The injured party may use a variety of ways, direct and indirect, to achieve this balance which may have varying results.

In their study of revenge in the workplace, Robert Bies and Thomas Tripp (2005), gave defining features that will help us understand what revenge is: it is provoked; it is evoked by many emotions; it has its unique rationality and morality; its emotions are controlled by socio-cognitive factors; and it takes a variety of forms.

Provocation Instigates Revenge

The quest for revenge always follows an act of provocation. If a person feels that another individual is obstructing him/her from obtaining the desired goal(s), the person will feel frustrated and, depending on the intensity of frustration, is likely to seek revenge. The provocation can also be a breach of organizational or social rules such as breaking a promise. Denigrating a person's status or sense of power or worth can also trigger the impulse for revenge.

Role of Emotions in Revenge

A sequence of our emotional feelings seems to accompany the experience of revenge. Following the injury, the injured person feels a heightened sense of violation. The person's "just-world hypothesis" is shattered. When a dear friend betrays our trust, we are left with a profound sense of violation accompanied by a sense of helplessness. We exhibit this sense through feelings of shock, confusion, and general disbelief of what happened. Feeling violated and helpless evoke very powerful emotions such as anger and rage. The person violated cannot shake the memory of the injury and is overwhelmed by a host of negative emotions that blind the intellect and inflame the desire to seek revenge. These revengeful emotions eventually become a part of the injured person's emotional makeup. The mental state of such a person was described by psychoanalyst David Werman as follows, "The desire for revenge can so pervade the inner world of an individual as to become an obsessive and destructive force in the person's life (Werman, 1993, p. 301).

Rationality & Morality of Revenge

How a person thinks about the causes of the initial injury determines whether a revenge impulse will be activated. In addition, whom the injured person blames and to what degree also influences whether or not the revenge motive will begin. The injured person is looking for answers to the question, "Why did the other person do this to me?" While trying to make sense of what happened, he/she is still experiencing a range of negative emotions. Will the "negative bias" of the injured person prevail? If it does, will the injurer be held totally responsible for the harm and wrongdoing while the injured person thinks of the injury as an attack against him/her? Or will there be circumstances that enable the injured person to look for "reasonable doubt" for the injurer, thereby lowering the intensity of the negative emotions? How the injured person answers these questions dictates whether revenge is justified as a way to defend oneself (rationality) and to do the right thing (morality).

Socio-Cognitive Factors

According to Robert Bies and Thomas Tripp, four primary factors affect the revenge motive. The first factor is exaggerating the injurer's negative intent by thinking that he/she meant to do what he/she did because he/she is a bad, mean, and wicked person. In the second factor, the victim <u>and</u> perpetrator each view him/herself as the victim. This is very likely to happen especially when the two sides have already engaged in the spiraling attack-counter attack cycle of revenge. In the third socio-cognitive factor, the injured ruminates over the harm and wrong done and becomes obsessed by the event, thereby strengthening the negative emotions and becoming more embittered and hateful toward the injurer. Defending one's ego is the fourth and final factor. Here the person lays the blame for what happened on someone else so the person can feel better about him/herself.

Variety of Forms for Revenge

Depending on the intensity and degree of harm done, revenge can take a variety of forms along the fight-flight continuum. The injured person may avoid any contact with the injurer. If they should meet by accident, the injured person ignores and does not acknowledge the injurer. Revenge can be in the form of retributive justice where the injured desires to see the injurer suffer a similar and equal suffering to his/hers. Revenge can also be direct or indirect, covert or overt.

Common in all the definitions above is the notion that revenge is personal, provoked, meditated, and involves meting out one's sense of justice, which often goes beyond the original intensity and degree of harm. Revengeful acts encapsulate the spectrum of aggressive behaviors. The perception of being wronged is at the core of this complex, powerful, and mysterious human dynamic of revenge. Let's now examine what revenge is not.

What Revenge Is Not

It is helpful to consider what revenge is not in order to deepen and sharpen our understanding of the defining characteristics of revenge and to indicate the differences between the concept of revenge with other constructs such as retaliation, hostility, reciprocity, retribution, incivility, bullying, or deviance, anger, and aggression.

Revenge is not the same as retaliation because in revenge the injured person usually mulls over the perceived hurtful episode(s) before taking any aggressive action against the alleged wrongdoer. In contrast, retaliatory acts often happen immediately after a hurtful event and try to deter the wrongdoer from repeating the offense. Moreover, revenge may not necessarily be rational while retaliation may be basically rational in its intent. On the other hand, revenge and retaliation may both deter future aggression, but revenge often sets the stage for a spiraling chain of aggression and counter-aggression.

Revenge is also different from retribution. Retribution acts are usually defined and sanctioned by the legal system of the state and, as such, have a limited intensity compared to acts of revenge where the intensity often exceeds the initial harm. Likewise, revenge is different from hostility in that revenge is motivated by a personal sense of being wronged while hostile acts may be undifferentiated feelings where the hostile person does not have a clear reason for his/her hostility. Also, a specific example would be helpful for several of these definitions] and acts toward others, regardless of whether the hostile person has been wronged or not.

Neither are revengeful acts the same as acts of reciprocity. In reciprocity the wronged party intends to give the offender "a taste of his/her own medicine," but the revengeful act is more than a "taste." Revengeful acts wield a greater degree of harm than the offender gave and go beyond the norms of reciprocity.

Revenge is not the same as incivility. Revenge is predicated on the perception of being wronged while incivility is motivated by feelings of competitiveness, inattentiveness, and disregard. For example, a person who is envious of his/her workmate's promotion may begin to ignore or act impolitely toward that person. In a similar vein, revenge is distinct from bullying which provokes aggression while revenge is an aggressive response to a provocation. Nor is revenge the same as deviance. Revenge is a reaction targeted toward an individual, a group, or an organization in response to a perceived injustice.

The relationship between revenge and anger is not very clear in the literature. In his 1993 master thesis, Paul Cardis indicated that the difference between revenge and anger lies in the fact that the emotion of anger fuels revenge, but revenge is not an emotion itself. Cardis also argued that revenge and aggression serve different functions, that is, aggression has offensive or defensive purposes while revenge is more deliberate and serves to alleviate one's emotional pain.

Although revenge is different from the constructs mentioned above, vengeful acts may be perceived as retaliatory, retributive, hostile, uncivil, deviant, and even reciprocal. Again, the primary motivation behind revenge-motivated aggression is a deep sense of grievance. The wronged person feels an intense desire and need to get even. Revenge may take a variety of forms including verbal, physical, or emotional and can be direct or indirect, covert or overt. The wronged party is consumed by his/her desire to set the scales of justice aright.

What then motivates humans to seek revenge? Why are we inclined to repay evil with evil? We'll explore that question next.

Why We Seek Revenge

According to a brain-imaging study published in the journal *Science* (2004), humans feel instinctive satisfaction when they punish a wrongdoer for what he/she did. The findings of this study justify the common saying, "Revenge is sweet." But is it? It may be initially, but does the sweetness last? Or, does the sweetness assuage the suffering inflicted by the wrong doer? Let's look at some of the explanations behind seeking revenge.

Fritz Heider offered four reasons are offered for seeking revenge. First, revenge is the injured person's attempt to change the offender's thoughts and beliefs. Plainly speaking, the injured person seeks to teach the injurer a lesson and to let him/her know that he/she can't go on offending with impunity. The injurer asserts him/herself in an attempt to restore a lost positive self-image. The following incident illustrates Heider's first rationale for revenge:

> Fred felt deeply wronged by the humiliating comments Chelsea made about him in front of their friends. This sense of humiliation left Fred feeling badly about himself and thinking of ways to get back at Chelsea. Fred knows which buttons to push to demean and denigrate Chelsea so that she will never again think of doing what she did to him. Fred also reasons that Chelsea and the rest of their friends will change their view of him as a humiliated Fred to a Fred who has a backbone, self-worth, and dignity. So Fred decides to have a get together the next day with friends including Chelsea so he can push Chelsea's buttons and put her down in front of everybody. Fred carried out his plan, which worked successfully. Seeing the defeated and vanquished look on Chelsea's face, Fred said to her, "I hope that this will teach you to never ever again mess with me."

Satisfying the injured person's sense of moral responsibility is the second reason for seeking revenge. Here, the wronged person feels compelled to seek revenge to fulfill social expectations and obligations. The injured person justifies his/her desire and need for revenge by believing it is sanctioned by societal norms, thereby de-personalizing the quest for revenge. That is, the avenger justifies his/her type and degree of revenge in terms of his/her obligation to conform to the dictates of the social forces, not those of the self. The "eye-for-an-eye" doctrine is a very good example of this type of revenge. Heider provides the following penetrating analysis of this type of revenge:

> [The avenger] typically feels righteous in his revenge because of the confounding of wish forces with ought forces. The need 'to get even,' to pay in kind, to hurt the enemy, may be so compelling that it assumes the character of a must, an ought force which is right and proper. (p. 273).

Revenge motivated by one's emotions toward the injurer is the third reason described for seeking revenge. The degree to which we like or dislike the injurer before the injury determines to a large extent the intensity of our feelings of revenge and the likelihood that we'll act on those feelings (Heider, 1958). If we feel positive toward the injurer before the offense, we may be less inclined to enact out revengeful thoughts and feelings, and vise versa.

Seeking revenge because we are angry is the fourth and final motive for revenge that Heider described. An angry person who feels deeply wronged does not concern himself/herself with changing the injurer's beliefs or bother with satisfying his/her moral obligation. Instead, the injured person's motivation to seek revenge is to express undirected aggression. That is, when the victim's undirected aggression is expressed, something unrelated to the original injury is damaged, destroyed, or injured. Undirected aggression is exemplified in the following statement by stand-up comic Rita Rudner quoted in Regina Barreca's 2005 book, *Sweet Revenge*, "I can't ask for money back that I loaned to a friend—the most I can do is, the next time I'm at their house, break something of approximate value" (p.1).

There are reasons for seeking revenge, but what type of revenge? Let's look at the different types of revenge.

Types of Revenge

Following are four types of revenge that Paul Cardis described in his 1993 master thesis: Behavioral revenge, cognitive revenge, affective revenge, and vicarious revenge.

Behavioral Revenge

In this type of revenge, the injured person acts upon his/her impulse to seek revenge for a perceived wrong. This is where one's cognitive plotting and planning are carried out against the enemy. The revenge plan may be a physical attack (beating, hitting, shooting), psychological (name-calling, put-downs) or social revenge plan (spreading rumors, character-assassination, social exclusion). The injured party will stop at nothing to make the offending party suffer.

Cognitive Revenge

The wronged person plots and plans revenge and even plays out the scenes of the revenge in the mind's eye. The person may get short-lived satisfaction out of the cognitive act where he/she shoots, maims, ridicules, etc. the injurer. The injured person may become so obsessed by the cognitive rehearsal of imagined and fantasized revengeful acts that he/she cannot concentrate on anything else. The thoughts of revenge are on the injured person's mind when he/she is eating, driving, working, studying, visiting with friends, shopping, or doing anything else. Revenge takes over the victim's life.

Affective Revenge

The injured cannot find it in his/her heart to wish the other person well. On the contrary, he/she is filled with poisonous and potent feelings of ill will toward the injurer. The revengeful affect, or emotion, is expressed in sentiments such as, "When I get the opportunity, I'll make him/her really suffer!" "I'll make him/her pay for what he/she did!"

Vicarious Revenge
When something bad befalls the person who wronged us, we get a sense of satisfaction. As the injured party, we delight in seeing misery and misfortune occur to our offenders. We bask in a perverse sense of pleasure when something awful happens to the person who injured us. We may think: "You deserve it fellow! You had it coming! I hope that hurt and hurt a lot!" In this type of revenge, we are not active agents, but we delight immensely when the injurer gets fired from his/her job, gets into an accident, is struck by lightening, gets severely sick, or suffers any other misfortune.

Three Categories of Revenge
Whether revenge is cognitive, affective, or behavioral, a person seeking revenge may exhibit one or a combination of three styles of revenge. The first is direct and open vindictiveness. The person may strike out at his/her opponent directly. An example of this style of revenge is an episode about a worker who put poison ivy on the toilet seat that his boss used (Described in Regina Barreca's 1995 book, Revenge is Sweet). It took two months for the boss to recover from the severe allergic reaction to the poison ivy. The worker lost his job and his claim of being victimized by mismanagement.

The second style is passive revenge which psychologist Karen Horney labeled as "self-effacing vindictiveness." The person projects the image of him/herself as the extremely good person who is always victimized and exploited by others. But the reality is that this person employs subversive and indirect acts of revenge. Examples include ways to discredit, attribute guilt to, and demoralize the other person.

The third and final style of revenge is what Regina Barreca called "detached vindictiveness." In this style the person seeks revenge by deliberately ignoring, disregarding, or forgetting the injurer and withholding praise, attention, and affection.

We see these three styles of revenge in action at the feeling, thinking, and acting level. The choice of one over the other depends on the perceived severity of the event that triggered revenge, the offender, and the revenge style of the offended.

Consequences of Revenge

The Ouroboros, an ancient symbol depicting a serpent or dragon devouring its own tail forming a circle, is used in Swenson's (2002) "Ouroboros Effect." It refers to the act of worsening something through attempts to make it better. The Ourboros symbol captures the cyclical and destructive nature of revenge, and the fact that revenge comes back to bite the avenger. Revenge has dire emotional, social and even physical consequences to the person seeking it, the person receiving it, and the people around it.

On the personal level, the seeker of revenge becomes overly obsessed by the thoughts, feelings, and wishes for revenge. This obsession consumes the entire being of the wronged person, draining him/her physically and emotionally. The person is wedded to revenge and becomes detached from the daily life events. He/she sees, hears, feels, smells, and senses revenge and only revenge. The harbored desire for revenge inflames the powerful emotions of hatred, anger, rage, and resentment in the innermost chambers of this person's heart. These emotions slowly spew and splash their toxin against every fiber of the person's personality. Repressed, these emotions are likely to lead to depression, hypertension, and other physical. Expressed, the fury is bound to wreak havoc on the innocent and guilty.

In addition, revenge forces the wronged party to stoop down to the level of the injurer in that he/she resorts to using similar methods to set the scales of justice aright. Commenting on the irrationality of this personal sense of righteous justice in his 1932 book, Ethical Relativity, Westermarck said, "ultimately, the seeker of revenge is often the victim of his own vengeance."

Moreover, the quest for and obsession with revenge do not allow the wounds of the injured to heal. With revenge, imagined, felt, or enacted, the wound opens wider and becomes deeper and fresher. The perpetual wound incapacitates and paralyzes the person's reason and heart, thereby beckoning the forces of vengeance to doctor the ever enlarging and deepening wound.

Maria's experience during her freshman year in college illustrates this pernicious consequence of revenge. Maria was deeply hurt when she found out that one of her dorm-mates put stolen items from other people's dorm rooms in Maria's room to make it look like Maria stole these items. One girl on the same floor told the Resident Assistant about items stolen and that Maria was a strong suspect. The RA went to Maria's room and confronted her about the issue. In shock and disbelief, Maria said to the RA, "I have no idea what you're talking about." The RA saw some of the specific stolen items under Maria's bed and when she asked Maria about what these items were and where they came from, Maria said, "These items aren't mine. I didn't put them there, and I have no idea who put them there. Somebody must be framing me!" Maria felt extremely hurt and angry and wanted to find out who did this to her and why. The RA reprimanded Maria and told she would be evicted if this happened again. A week passed and Maria found out who the culprit was. It was her rival in the student government body who was very jealous of Maria's popularity and leadership skills and wanted to see Maria humiliated and discredited.

Maria could not stop thinking about the person who wanted to ruin her reputation and soon gave in to thoughts, plots, and plans of getting even. Maria spent the rest of her freshman year obsessed with getting back at her dorm-mate. The more she thought about what she did to her, the angrier she got. Maria did not miss any opportunity to speak ill of and demonize the dorm-mate. One day, the dam of rage within Maria exploded, unleashing its fury unto the dorm-mate. Maria went to the dorm-mate's room and started beating and kicking on her relentlessly. The campus police were called and Maria was arrested and subsequently expelled from the dorm. Maria's initial hurt was only made worse by her attempts at exacting a "just" price for the injustice the dorm-mate caused her. Her wound began to heal when she and dorm-mate went through a semester-long, dorm-sponsored conflict resolution and the two expressed their feelings about each other. The two began to work out their differences, apologized to one another, and vowed to put an end to the past and begin a new chapter in their relationship.

As Maria's story suggests, an attack most always provokes a counter attack. Unless something is done about it, the cycle of revenge escalates and puts in motion what has been called "a competition in cruelty."

The consequences of revenge not only include souring the relationship with the other person involved but possibly with their relatives, friends, co-workers, and other people in their social spheres. The acts of revenge often spillover beyond the parameters of the players involved in this vicious game. In a family where the revenge starts between the parents, its flames soon engulf the children, and may drag in extended family members and friends. Unless contained, the deleterious and almost intractable effects of revenge will threaten harmony and peace in the family, workplace, and community.

Alternatives to Revenge

Numerous alternatives to revenge include: ignoring the person who injured us, seeking advice from a professional helper, talking to a friend, venting out by talking to anyone who will listen to us, trying to talk directly with the injurer, seeking resolution through mediation, keeping oneself busy and re-channeling time and energy into more productive activities such as community volunteer work, or working through the pain and forgiveness to find inner release from revenge and the negative emotions that sustain it. In his 1984 doctoral dissertation, Droll pointed out that six potential rewards await those who forgive: (1) helps to avoid the costs of revenge; (2) increases feelings of self-esteem; (3) decreases the problem of increasing hostilities; (4) decreases negative feelings such as anger, rage, and resentment; and (6) allows the possibility to restore the broken relationship. For example, research on forgiveness (Trainer,1981) in the context of divorce showed that the intrinsic forgivers (those characterized by benevolent behavior and an inner change in attitudes and feelings toward the offender) tended to have less self-defeating behaviors, gained more personal power over their hostile impulses, were more self-accepting, made their anger subside, and overcame their desire for revenge.

Summary & Conclusion

Revenge is a response to a perceived injustice with a goal of making the offender suffer to the degree of harm he/she caused. A person can seek revenge actively or passively and may derive short-lived feelings. But the appetite for revenge is insatiable, and its consequences are often destructive. Consumed by revenge, a person depletes his/her energy and can get sick both physically and emotionally. The person would be much better off if he/she spent the time and energy not on revenge but on more effective and healthful ways to improve life and relationships with others. Instead of constantly entertaining and enacting thoughts of revenge, a person may decide to assess the costs and benefits of revenge and then look for a better alternative. For some people, the alternative may be to ignore the offender altogether, to seek professional help or the counsel of a trusted friend, to have someone mediate the conflict, or to forgive the wrong doer. The path of forgiveness can be long and painful, but the pain one endures during the process of forgiveness has the paradoxical effect of freeing him/her from the pain and also makes it possible for the injured and injurer to repair their fractured relationship. The next chapters will help you in your forgiveness quest.

Footnote:

When a grandson told of his anger at a schoolmate who had done him an injustice, his grandfather said, "Let me tell you a story.

"I, too, have felt a great hate for those who have taken so much, with no sorrow for what they do. But, hate wears you down and does not hurt your enemy. It is like taking poison and wishing your enemy would die. I have struggled with these feelings many times.

"It is as if there are two wolves inside me: one is good and does no harm. He lives in harmony with all around him and does not take offense when no offense was intended. He will only fight when it is right to do so, and in the right way.

"But the other wolf is full of anger. The littlest thing will set him into a fit of temper. He fights with everyone, all the time, for no reason. He cannot think because his anger and hate are so great.

"It is hard to live with these two wolves inside me, for both of them try to dominate my spirit."

The boy looked intently into his grandfather's eyes and asked, "Which one wins, Grandfather?"

The grandfather solemnly replied, "The one I feed."

Comment:

The battle is largely within. Nothing that lives can live without being fed. This is true whether we're talking about our physical, mental, emotional, or spiritual lives. A body requires nourishment. Our thoughts require some form of intention. Our emotions require some form of initiative. Our spirit must long for something just beyond its reach.

Likewise, forgiveness and un-forgiveness must be fed. They are both fed with everything we are as physical and psychological beings. We choose what we will use to feed, nourish, and sustain these two conditions in life. Like two wolves, they fight for the territory of our hearts. The battle is ceaseless. Only one wolf will win each of the battles for its life and ours.

We can feed an injury by playing the incident over and over again. Relentlessly touching and reopening the wound is painful. We are intent upon remaining angry and resentful. Or, we can try to understand why we feel so hurt and uncompromising. Each attitude influences the wolf we feed. Which one is winning in your life?

CHAPTER FOUR

Gateway One: Awareness of the Injury

Making Contact: We belong to one another.

Story:

AND THEY CALL some of these people "retarded. A few years ago, at the Seattle Special Olympics, nine contestants, all physically or mentally disabled, assembled at the starting line for the 100-yard dash. At the gun, they all started out, not exactly in a dash, but with a relish to run the race to the finish and win. All, that is, except one little boy who stumbled on the asphalt, tumbled over a couple of times, and began to cry. The other eight heard the boy cry. They slowed down and looked back. Then they all turned around and went back...every one of them. One girl with Down's Syndrome bent down and kissed him and said, "This will make it better." Then all nine linked arms and walked together to the finish line.

Everyone in the stadium stood, and the cheering went on for several minutes. People who were there are still telling the story today. Why? Because deep down we know this one thing: What matters in this life is more than winning for ourselves. What matters in this life is helping others win, even it if means slowing down and changing our course.

Comment:

In a competitive society and under competitive conditions, it is not natural to go back and rescue a fallen comrade. Nor is it natural to fall, have no one return to help, and then forgive them for their indifference or insensitivity.

We fall often in life and need someone to take our hand and help us up. Forgiveness is often about going back to the hurtful situation. The distance back will depend upon how far we have run away from those who hurt us or let us down. The distance back is less formidable if our heart takes charge and tells us life is really about walking together. Everyone wins when we realize the race is not a contest, but an opportunity to finish where we started out together.

Cuts and bruises in life are common physical ailments that we often simply treat with a Band-Aid to minimize the pain. We can repress the pain as we get involved in other things and distance ourselves from the original source of the hurt. These cuts and bruises gradually heal. We expect and can see that things are getting better. This healing creates hopeful prospects that recovery will be complete.

Psychological injury and treatment are sometimes like physical injury. Usually, we try to present our best self to the world, and we hope to receive acceptance and approval in return. Yet, at times we are rebuffed and rejected. We experience cuts and bruises to our sense of importance and feeling/being worthwhile. Our self-esteem is shaken by something someone says or does. We are confronted with an aspect of ourselves that we may not like to admit or may have hoped others would not notice.

At other times we are psychologically scolded or reprimanded for intruding upon the psychological space of another. We have created some trouble in their world and they retaliate in some way. The effects are similar to those instances when our efforts are misinterpreted or underappreciated—it makes us feel less good about ourselves as persons. We sometimes feel less kindly toward those who make us feel this way.

We often treat psychological cuts or bruises with Band-Aids, too. In some instances the Band-Aid can become a permanent rather than a temporary solution. We neglect to occasionally look at the wound and remove the Band-Aid in favor of full exposure to the world. Ego hurts are often protected long after the injury. By using techniques of self-deception, people can distance themselves from the pain and create an illusion that things are okay or at least getting better. While illusions helps restore our pseudo-good health, the injury has only been treated with irrational and deceptive adjustments designed to distort reality and eliminate feelings of unworthiness.

A brief look at these "defense mechanisms" can help you discover ways you may have chosen to deal with the intrapersonal and interpersonal pain in your life.

Roadblocks to Awareness: Signs of Self- Deception

<u>Rationalization</u> involves manufacturing ostensible reasons to justify interpretations of hurtful actions and experiences. For example, if someone does not return your telephone calls, you may suspect the person does not take you very seriously and feel you've been snubbed. Or, you might reason that the person has been exceedingly busy. This is a generous and kindly interpretation that preserves your sense of possessing these virtues (giving the person the benefit of the doubt to maintain the kindly attitude you admire about yourself), or it may permit you to view the person as unreliable and irresponsible (lacking qualities that you hold dear and attribute to yourself.)

<u>Compensation</u> serves to counterbalance the excruciating pain of an injury by indulging in highly pleasurable activities. People often rebound from the distress of losing a loving relationship by throwing themselves into their work. The self-satisfaction that accompanies achievement or the accolades from colleagues may be regarded as a suitable substitute for the pleasure of the earlier relationship. We operate as though the two sources of satisfaction are interchangeable—one can compensate for the other. Actually, there are seldom satisfying substitutes for those things that really matter in life. The difference between the compensatory activity and the original relationship becomes a nagging feeling that things are not all right. The missing elements of the preferred relationship are experienced as a longing for something more.

<u>Repression</u> is employed to bury painful feelings from asserting themselves. You refuse to think the unthinkable, and refrain from doing the forbidden. Often repression is used to hide a truth about oneself or others that would be

difficult to accept. It is often used to deal with "supposed to" and "ought to." "My parents were supposed to love me and be good to me. I dare not experience the pain of contrary notions about this relationship. Doing so could undermine my respect for them." Or, "I ought to love my parents, for they are my parents and warrant my affection. Exposing myself to contradictory notions would destroy my respect for myself."

Shoulds and oughts are generally embedded in cultural norms and family expectations as principles to uphold and to live by. Because pain is associated with departing from these standards, we might repress evidence that refutes our departure from the so-called ideal. Much psychic energy is invested in keeping the pain submerged below the surface of our awareness. But in our subconscious, the pain persists and assumes a dynamic state that influences our behaviors.

<u>Regression</u> involves a return to less mature patterns of behavior to lessen the pain associated with an experience we cannot handle. If a person cannot imagine being sufficient to handle the demands of the situation, he/she may retreat to a behavior that makes the person feel more confident and self-assured. Expecting less and doing less salvage the pain of feeling inept and impotent. While there's no longer a threat to the self-esteem, the individual is now robbed of an opportunity for growth. Working through the pain would result in new behavior and an enlarged capacity to meet other challenges.

<u>Projection</u> enables us to get relief from pain by attributing the cause to the external world. Instead of saying, "I am unforgiving," one can say, "This person refused to accept forgiveness or deliberately behaves in ways to make it impossible for me to be forgiving." To accept responsibility for being unforgiving would require examining our own mistakes, facing the truth about us. Instead, we assign blame to someone else and feel justified in our internal desire to be unforgiving. The plausible excuses and alibis we construct, distorting the truth to avoid punishing ourselves for reprehensible behavior, make projection a very popular way to alienate the need to forgive while consoling ourselves with the rightness of our actions.

<u>Reaction Formation</u> seeks to conceal unforgiving by appropriating and extending exaggerated forgiveness behavior. The virtue of forgiveness is compulsively expressed to hide the accusation of unforgiving. Forgiveness becomes extravagant, ostentatious, and affected. Often others see it as pretense because it is so overdone.

<u>Fixation</u> at a certain stage in the forgiveness process is based on assessing the hazards and hardships that lie ahead such as insecurity, failure, and punishment. Some of us may feel unable to deal with the demands of experiencing and expressing forgiveness. If we do not know what to do and/or what to say, we may anticipate a painful outcome. This is one impetus for fear of failure. Anticipating failure contributes to reticence, if not resistance, to taking the steps toward forgiveness. Threats to our self-esteem and fear of punishment are also powerful inducements to play it safe. What if the person who is to be the object of forgiveness refuses it? Forgiveness contributes to our personal vulnerability; it opens us to rejection. Playing it safe, staying put, protecting ourselves seem a better road to take when weighed against the possible risks of taking a chance. However, consider that the pain we experience when we confront our pain is liberating, while the pain we experience when we choose to hold on to our pain is enslaving.

Resistance to Change: Efforts to Control the Pain

Defense mechanisms let us deceive ourselves and help us preserve a self we can at least endure and hopefully respect. They serve as a safety net so we don't have a falling out with ourselves. Defense mechanisms also give us a way to react to deep pain that we didn't do anything to deserve. For example, self-deception is a form of resistance to change to preserve our position by seeking validation for it. We choose behaviors not to control ourselves, as in the case of defense mechanisms, but to control others. The purpose remains the same: defending ourselves against change and finding comfort in doing so.

Additional Obstacles/Impediments to Experiencing the Pain

We spend huge sums of money to get relief from pain, yet exercise enthusiasts often proclaim, "No pain, no gain." Without subjecting the body to some pain, there cannot be any growth toward physical wellness. We also avoid psychological pain and spend vast amounts of money to receive relief. Yet, many resist facing the source of their pain. Others refuse to accept or apply the remedy. Resisting the expression of painful feelings is viewed as another implicit reality.

The analogous relationship between physical and psychological pain is not lost in our experience of living. Both procedures work in tandem. Physical pain is often the precursor to psychological pain. Likewise, psychological pain is frequently the precursor to physical pain. Abnormality in either area contributes to a tension often experienced as pain in the other. Even though we seek ways to unify our experiences of living, we actually choose pain in an effort to control it and preserve our position. Instead, generally the pain gets worse. Rather than dealing directly with the events responsible for our pain, we seek indirect remedies that show promise of reducing the pain while leaving the situation unchanged.

William Glasser (Control Theory) offers several explanations for our resistance to change. He asserts that we frequently choose misery in order to:

1) keep 'angering' under control
2) get others to help us
3) excuse our unwillingness to do something more
4) gain powerful control

We choose painful feeling behaviors to regain control over a situation that we do not wish to acknowledge and/or do not want to face head-on. But the painful feelings we choose negate our growing towards a solution to the problem we wish to avoid. Let us examine each of these pain-perpetuating strategies we use to mask or resist the pain of positioning ourselves to forgive.

Keeping Angering Under Control

Glasser deliberately selects a verb rather than a noun to express an emotion. Rather than being angry, we are angering. We are not deprived, we are depriving. The verb connotes a choice. Anger does not just happen to us. We choose to be angry. When we accept this proposition, we can learn to accept responsibility for managing our emotions. Angering is a counterproductive emotion. It offends people; it alienates both self and others. People fight back or refuse to be drawn into anger.

Depressing is a much more effective way to move others into action. Everyone has been discouraged, disillusioned, and defeated. Everyone has reached out for sympathy and known the comfort of companionship. This experience creates a readiness to reach out to others. While depressing can be painful, it does not have the destructive drawbacks of angering. Those who see someone giving up on themselves try to let us know they have not. They will go out of their way to minister to us. The pain of depressing is offset by control over others which makes us feel better, but the relief is short-lived. Eventually we must acknowledge that depressing is chosen and we must learn new behaviors to replace these painful feelings.

Getting Others to Help Us

Choosing misery, expressed as various forms of depressing, need, and melancholy is powerful help-getting behavior. These are passive ways to ask for help that reduce the threat of being rejected when directly asking for help.

Asking for help is in itself a painful experience. Our culture teaches us to be competent and independent. Seeking help suggests a lack of competence and contributes to dependence. When our self-esteem is at stake, it seems better to deny that we need help than fall prey to an emotion of helplessness.

Only after we can assume responsibility for our emotions, viewing them as a choice we make, can we begin to look for better behavior. More responsible behavior is free of excuses. More hopeful behavior is an outgrowth of coming to terms with a dreadful situation.

Excusing Our Unwillingness to do Something More

Excuses generally originate in our feelings of weakness. We cannot imagine making choices that demand strength or action. We prefer to let others assume responsibility and rescue us from our feelings. How can we, feeling as we do, expect anything more? How can they, seeing us in misery, expect anything less?

Excuses are also an outgrowth of fear of failure. The stretch to grasp the possibilities is curtailed by fear of the unknown and/or fear of disaster/disappointment. We are convinced the situation calls for more than we feel capable of giving. We become anxious and apprehensive about a complete breakdown, so we exonerate ourselves with excuses. We find it painful to get started when we doubt our ability to change an unsatisfactory situation or when we are apprehensive about others' response. We excuse ourselves saying, "At least while engaged in miserying behavior people will help me out. What they do for me reduces what I need to do for myself."

Protecting ourselves from ourselves can become a full-time job. We adopt routines for keeping our fears of inadequacy under control. The psychological energy we invest in avoidance behavior depletes our reservoir of strength. While the routines are self-defeating in the long-run, they do have the appeal of an easy way out. We accept less from life than we desire or deserve.

To Gain Powerful Control

When we feel out-of-control, we often employ drastic and dramatic ways to regain control. We may feel like an automobile driver negotiating a slippery roadway, losing control of the car, and then trying to turn against the skid to regain control. When we feel control slipping away, we frantically try to choose our most capable behavior although it may not be sufficient to the situation. In our desperate attempt to find a safe haven from the painful results of our choices, we may choose gaining control without regard to the long-term consequences.

If we're successful in gaining control, we remain safe in the knowledge that others are drawn into the fray and we don't have to do anything new. Under these conditions, there is no possibility of making mistakes or taking more effective choices. However, taking control with dependence on others contributes to growth-inhibiting behaviors and eventually reduces our options when life circumstances change. Giving up control, even painful control, is accompanied by uncertainty and trepidation. Only slowly and painfully can we relinquish what has become a psychological crutch and an escape from a reality we refuse to acknowledge.

Taking Responsibility for Our Feelings

Feelings are a choice. Only when we accept this premise can we begin to choose behaviors with the potential for creating the feelings we want. While it's helpful to understand the dynamics of defense mechanisms, we also need an awareness of the consequences of unforgiving. These feelings and behaviors can also provide compelling reasons to forgive. Doris Donnelly, in her fine book titled <u>Learning to Forgive</u>, cites and discusses ten unpleasant and unhealthy personal consequences of refusing to forgive, namely:

1) being led by anger, pain, or hatred;
2) being directed by negative memories;
3) unable to act freely;
4) need to keep a controlling grasp on situations and people;
5) being pressured by lives of tension and stress;
6) shortened lives;
7) strained relations with others;
8) weakened relationship with God;
9) living with feelings of little self-control;
10) living with unrelieved guilt.

Anger
When anger takes hold of your hand, it takes you to the threshold of bitterness and resentment. Dwelling on the injustices drags you across the landscape of contempt. Unforgiving dwells on revenge, on getting even. You may be consumed with inflicting pain upon another. However, this unremitting desire to risk retaliation often claims the heart and soul of the avenger.

Negative Memories
Whenever someone is tyrannized by negative emotions, no healing can occur. Painful memories are too heavy a burden to carry alone. Ceaseless efforts to get rid of these negative emotions contribute to all forms of ill-will. When people are fueled by reactions to their ill-will, they often continue an endless cycle of striking out and striking down. The forces of evil wreak havoc with their sense of compassion and deprive them of consolation.

Unable to Act Freely
Shackled by negative emotions, all of a person's energies are thrown into validating the negative emotion. People in this situation become captive to a pride that serves to justify these feelings and actions and a self-pity that refuses to look within and beyond to empathize with the target of these emotions. There can be no peace without the courage and boldness to surrender. There can be no happiness without kindness wrapped in mercy. Crippling servitude is the choice of those who choose to be prisoners of their negative emotions.

Controlling Others
As we noted earlier, misery may be chosen to control others or to permit others to control us. While the squeaky wheel may get the grease, this is usually a costly way to receive service from others. It may be interpreted as greedy and selfish, and that eventually lead to ostracism from the group. This could

isolate and alienate them from the mainstream of life, with few social interactions. To be free of this control, the individual must free others and him/herself from the yoke of unforgiving.

Pressures

Our bodies are not immune from the stress and tension associated with negative emotions. We pay the price in all sorts of real and imagined illnesses. The physical manifestations—diarrhea, headaches, high blood pressure, chest pains, muscle spasms, colitis, insomnia, ulcers, asthma, and exhaustion—are just a few disorders that can be attributed to the negative emotions associated with unforgiving. Our bodies cannot withstand the continuous onslaught of the clenched fist.

Our negative self-talk may also magnify the hurt and intensify feelings. There is no respite from these emotions and yet we get only incomplete satisfaction when expressing them. There is a relentless need to get even without a clear sense of what this might entail. At times we may yield grudgingly to the need to forgive, but with this attitude, aggravation and irritability persist. A backlash of meanness and maliciousness continues to take its internal toll.

Shorter Lives

Emotional stress and tensions are registered in all parts of the body. When the body and the psyche engage in constant struggle, the accumulation of these detrimental consequences shortens the life span. Small struggles become big battles. Battles become all-out wars. A war is seldom won, and certainly not without great cost—the possible shortening of your life.

Personal Distancing

Strained relationships are outgrowths of combatant attitudes and hostile behaviors that increase the pressure with hateful feelings. These touch old wounds and prevent healing. Some people may resort to physical and psychological distancing behaviors, which can minimize the risks and reduce vulnerability. The wounds that remain are a constant reminder of the dangers of further injury.

Spiritual Distancing

When we are not one with our neighbors, we cannot be at one with God. When we cannot love those who we can see, how can we love God who we cannot see? Our lack of forgiveness reveals God's inability to work in our lives. Were we fully present to Him, we would be able to love those He loves. Hurt separates and keeps others at arm's length, while love embraces. But, we cannot embrace anyone with our arms crossed or our feet planted in a hostile, unbending, stiff-necked posture. Forgiveness reaches out. A strong relationship with God nurtures the inclinations to love and strengthens the desire for healing.

Lack of Self Control

Our self-worth is grounded in relationships that make us distinctive from others. As we grow toward a definition of self, we come to hold certain opinions and truths about ourselves, which we act upon each day. Viewing us as virtuous, forgiving, and loving contributes to positive feelings of self-esteem. Regarding ourselves as hateful and vindictive contradicts our beliefs about ourselves. We feel less worthy of others' positive regard and we suffer the isolation and loneliness of being separated from the self we would like to be. We lack the wholeness that makes us feel complete, at least as persons who are in the process of seeking the fullness of life.

Unrelieved Guilt

We feel guilty when we shortchange ourselves and others. We know that we owe more to ourselves and to others. The disparity between what is and what can be haunts us. We feel the pangs of guilt because we do not measure up to our ideals. Guilt seeks changes in what we believe to be possible and what we are doing about it. Bridging the gap between the two can be a liberating experience and the impetus for self-forgiveness and the forgiveness of others. But, being guilty of unforgiving can hopelessly imprison us for life.

Conclusion

Many roadblocks get in the way of forgiveness, and there are many unfortunate consequences for not forgiving. When we weigh them in the scales of love and mercy, the impediments become less formidable, but the consequences are more stultifying. Given this awareness, we are at least prepared to entertain the possibilities of forgiveness. We may be willing to begin using our understanding to take another look at our pain, even to experience it more fully, so we can compare holding on to it with letting go of it.

Footnote:

How High Can You Jump?

Fleas are trained by putting them in a cardboard box with a top on it. The insects will jump up and hit the top of the cardboard box repeatedly. As this jumping continues, however, something becomes obvious: The fleas continue to jump – but no longer high enough to hit the top. The undoubtedly painful experience of banging their tiny heads on the box top inspires them to decrease the height of their jump.

When you take off the lid, the fleas continue to jump, but they don't jump out of the box. They don't jump out because they can't. They have conditioned themselves to jump only so high.

People do the same thing, don't they? They hold themselves back and never reach their potential. Just like the fleas, they fail to jump higher – thinking they're doing all they can.

—Adapted from the *30 Best Inspiring Anecdotes of All Time.*

Comment:

Defense mechanisms condition us to believe we are doing all we can do. If we were to do otherwise, it would be too painful. It would be like hitting your head against a self-imposed ceiling.

CHAPTER FIVE

Gateway Two: Experience the Pain

Making Contact: Pain as a claim and an aim.

Story:

A MAN WAS getting a haircut prior to a trip to Rome. He mentioned the trip to his barber who responded, "Rome? Why would anyone want to go there? It's crowded, dirty, and full of Italians. You're crazy to go to Rome. So, how are you getting there?"

"We're taking TWA," was the reply. "We got a great rate!"

"TWA?" exclaimed the barber. "That's a terrible airline. Their planes are old, their flight attendants are ugly, and they're always late. So, where are you staying in Rome?"

"We'll be at the downtown International Marriott."

"That dump! That's the worst hotel in the city. The rooms are small, the service is surly, and they're overpriced. So, whatcha doing when you get there?"

"We're going to go to see the Vatican and we hope to see the Pope."

"That's rich," laughed the barber. "You and a million other people trying to see him. He'll look the size of an ant from where you stand. Boy, good luck on this lousy trip of yours. You're going to need it."

A month later, the man again came in for his regular haircut. The barber asked him about his trip to Rome.

"It was wonderful," explained the man. "Not only were we on time in one of TWA's brand new planes, but it was overbooked and they bumped us up to first class. The food and wine were wonderful, and I had a beautiful 28-year-old stewardess who waited on me hand and foot.

And the hotel….it was great! They'd just finished a $25 million remodeling job and now it's the finest hotel in the city. They, too, were overbooked, so they apologized and gave us the presidential suite at no extra charge!"

"Well," muttered the barber, "I know you didn't get to see the pope."

"Actually, we were quite lucky, for as we toured the Vatican, a Swiss Guard tapped me on the shoulder and explained that the pope likes to personally meet some of the visitors, and if I'd be so kind as to step into his private room and wait, the pope would personally greet me. Sure enough, five minutes later the pope walked through the door and shook my hand! I knelt down as he spoke a few words to me."

"Really?" asked the Barber. "What'd he say?"

"He said, 'Where'd you get that lousy haircut?'"

Comment:

Revenge is a powerful pain reliever. After being hurt, we cunningly wait for an opportunity to get our pound of flesh. Sometimes it is a matter of one-upmanship. We cannot resist a one-liner (often the one we wished we had thought of at the time) that cuts to the core. We swoop down like an eagle seeking its prey. With one fell swoop we satisfy the urge to get even.

However, getting even is a math-emotional construct rather than an emotionally driven idea. It is not easy to balance an equation with a condition of the heart. Yet this weightless condition can feel like a heavy burden. We often begin by measuring out the pain like a boxer sparring with his opponent. At the outset, good footwork and a few good jabs may feel good but hardly satisfy. Eventually the boxer wants to square off and deliver a knock-out punch. Victory is standing back in the corner after the other person hits the mat. He had it coming.

For the boxer, it is then a matter of getting back to a training regimen to be ready to accept and deliver pain. This thinking and the corresponding practices reveal the dark side of dealing with pain. The satisfaction is as temporary as the amount of time it takes to deliver the zinger. Instead, using the pain to begin thinking about non-combative approaches may be risky but does have the potential for ending the cycle of pain exchange.

Suffering is a normal and painful experience of living. We know what it is like to be broken down and broken-hearted. We learn how to put our lives back together after broken promises and broken relationships have temporarily incapacitated us with an embittered spirit. We have been wounded, cut down, sharply rebuked, ripped apart, and sliced to the bone. We know what it is like to be reduced to nothing, to come up short, and dissolved into tears. Life can be harsh; there is no escape from adversity. We are beset with trials, tribulations, and tragedy. Sometimes we deal with them with quiet resignation, sometimes with spirited resistance, and other times with fuming indignation. Sometimes we learn resilience and bounce back from fatalism and futility. We refuse to take life lying down. Painful as life can be, we manage to recuperate and take up life where we left off. We learn that the fullest possession of life includes a daring sensitivity and courageous acceptance of pain. We go on.

Suffering can be redemptive. We can either stretch or shrink before it. We can be a woeful spirit and chronic complainer, or, we can use suffering to re-imagine our goals, realign our priorities, rekindle our passion, and increase our endurance. We can curse life as dreary and dreadful, or regard adversity as a temporary setback. Rather than being disarmed by pain and agonizing about it, we can boldly and bravely refuse to be captive to our suffering. Even in our darkest hour we can find light if we believe there is something illuminating about suffering and something transformative about its power.

Forgiving-the prospect and promise-can be fraught with suffering. Forgiving can be a harsh recognition of our own culpability. We can easily be hijacked by casting the blame elsewhere. "It was not my fault and I refuse to believe it is." Or, we might actually be convinced that we are not culpable and think, "This is just another painful instance where I am a victim of another person's insensitivity or ineptness." Regardless of the questionable or faulty attributions, we must deal with the opposition here or there.

Having waxed somewhat philosophically about suffering and pain, let us re-enter the process of forgiveness using the context and content of the previous chapter. Beginning there we remind ourselves that we experience the world and act on it with our five senses by doing, thinking, and feeling. These actions are mediated and regulated by voluntary and involuntary physiological mechanisms. When we look back upon an experience we are likely to focus on one or more of these four sensory related components of a complete behavior. We might emphasize what we were thinking, how we were feeling, or what we were doing. We are likely to describe the physiology of one or more of these behaviors. The previous chapter emphasized the thinking and doing behaviors we might use to avoid, bury, or mask feeling behaviors. We examined the ways thinking and doing behaviors could be used to manage and control painful feelings. We also learned about some of the detrimental outcomes of substituting thinking and doing behaviors for feeling behaviors.

As you read the last chapter, you decided it was better to face your problem head-on, especially if you've found relying on thinking and doing behaviors is not enough. Even with this decision, you may continue to experience periodic bouts of feeling down on life and yourself. You may have a nagging feeling that something is terribly wrong or missing in your life, but you are beginning to wonder what would make things better. Maybe, just maybe, you must face something in your life you have refused to face. It may be time to face the consequences of unforgiving, to understand that the pain of saying "no" to someone is just as bad as withholding a "yes" to yourself.

Saying "yes" to you means giving yourself permission to experience a full measure of pain. It means reliving an event without recourse to the thinking and doing behaviors that you've used to protect yourself from painful feeling behaviors. Unguarded and vulnerable, you surrender to the full impact of the original event. You allow the pain to spill out into all the crevices of your heart. Each beat of your heart pumps the pain into your system. The pain fills you with agony, anger, indignity, and indignation. Dread, doubt, and fear may overwhelm you.

Experience the Pain

The anger and fear you feel are powerful emotions. Their counterparts are found in all kinds of painful feeling behaviors, such as bitterness, rage, scorn, hate, anxiousness, and panic. These painful feeling behaviors harbor the elements of an event you remember but have not fully experienced. Only by returning to all elements of the event can you begin to relive the pain and grapple with the original choices you made to deal with it— choices that have coalesced into an inability to forgive.

Reliving the experience and responding to the questions that follow will resurrect the pain as you now look back at the event with a more dispassionate view. You can move cautiously and then deftly step along the path towards recovery as you gain the strength of mind and spirit. Dwell on the answer to each question until you can feel the hurt, until you can relive the crippling emotions. You must eventually surrender this pain in order to make space for forgiveness, for letting love enter the unoccupied space and opening the door to forgiveness.

When and What Happened?

Begin by recreating the context for the episode by recalling all of the circumstances that placed you in the clutches of unforgiving. Remember the context as a history of events that preceded the feelings that, "this is the last straw" or "I have had it up to here." After all, this is only one of a series of offensive experiences. You may have been embarrassed, shamed, or humiliated. You have had your sense of self-worth and self-esteem stripped. Whether fight or flight, whether a series of events or a single event, you live the consequences as a deeply personal experience.

Even the season, month of the year, day of the week, time of the day or night could contribute to the significance you attribute to this event. The dizzy pace of the Christmas season, a bitter January, the "Thank God it's Friday," or the fatigue at the end of a day can elevate and magnify the emotional features of the event. They can also color an event as distressing, disheartening, or devastating. All of these aspects of an event can markedly influence your capacity to forgive.

Who was the Culprit?
As you recall the context, think of the other people who were present. Their participation, whether it is active or passive, probably fueled the intensity of your feelings. Picture each person, and recall how he or she looked and what he or she said. Retrace the feelings associated with the pictures. Draw the feelings of their involvement as you re-experience the event.

Now, recall who stepped into this context as the antagonist! Who is the target of your animosity or shame? This person stands at center stage in the drama and further intensifies feelings of anger. You feel the pain more profoundly because you can reinstate the images and accompanying emotions. Some things about this person—what he says, how he says it, how she looks, what she does—amplify and intensify the memories as your emotions return to the surface.

How has this person hurt you? What part of you is in pain? Is it the part of you that feels deprived of something? Has something been taken from you that cannot never be replaced? The person who took it does not appreciate its value, may have discarded it like an old shoe or may have even celebrated his good fortune. Or, is the pain due to having to accept something you neither want nor are fully equipped to take on? You may feel the burden of additional responsibility. Yet, the other person escaped the consequences of his action. While his life goes on as though nothing happened, your life will never be the same.

What Motives?
What explanations and justifications do you muster on behalf of your unforgiving? They undoubtedly included attributions about the motive of the offending party. When you regard the motive as deliberate and unprovoked, you feel even more justification to hang onto your anger. When you see the person as inconsiderate and possibly unrepentant, your hurt continues although the provocations may have been unintentional and inadvertent. You may never have a satisfying answer to why someone would inflict so much pain upon you. However, until you deal with the pain in the absence of motives, you will keep a gnawing need for retaliation.

What Response?

Accepting the pain without recourse to inflicting a portion of it on another is the only clear path to freedom. Take on the entire pain as though you are the only one who can gather it, mold it into a ball, and throw it into the outer reaches of the universe. You now find you have used the pain to defend yourself against forgiveness. The pain is real, but much of what sustains it is imagined. Forgiveness absorbs pain like a sponge. It soaks up the pain that has permeated the very essence of who you are and how you live your life.

Now you must deal with the tangible consequences of the actions of the person(s) you refuse to forgive. The consequences are painful demands of being something or somebody you are not. They generally mean having to take on something difficult or having to do without something valued. The presence or absence of something is a painful reminder of the way(s) you have been victimized. You have lost control over some important aspects of living. You can no longer count on someone to be there for you or cannot count on yourself to be there for yourself. You struggle to recapture a part of life taken from you. You must manage the actual pain and unrealized aims and aspirations.

Now it is time to regain control by developing a new set of thinking behaviors and using them to replace the feeling behaviors that justified unforgiving. New ways of thinking can change old ways of feeling.

Thoughts drawn together and used to muster resolve can lead to action steps that reinforce a decision to forgive. The complementary components of all behaviors make what seemed impossible become possible. The specific action steps toward forgiveness will be described in the next chapter. Before we talk about them, let's look back at the pervasiveness of several thinking behaviors.

Persuasion, building an argument to justify a position or stance, is often the prelude to a corresponding action. Can I persuade myself to be forgiving? Lewis Smedes, the author of Forgive and Forget, offers four reasons to become a forgiving person: Forgiving makes life easier; forgiving is a better risk; forgiving is stronger; and forgiving fits faulty people. Each reason should help dissolve the defense mechanisms used to exonerate us from the stubbornness and guilt of unforgiving. Each reason should suggest something we can do to bring the fruits of forgiveness to the hurtful person(s).

Forgiving Makes Life Easier

Hanging on to the memories of the hurtful situation prolongs the painful feelings and perpetuates the corresponding resentful feeling behaviors. Life becomes burdensome under the sheer weight of a perceived injustice. One daily wears a yoke of wrongs and is led away from forgiveness by feelings of unfairness.

Fairness is an elusive concept and can be an insidious drawback to forgiveness. It is a cruel hoax to believe fairness can even a score. Trying to achieve a balance in the distribution of pain is an exercise in futility. It either results in a constant exchange of retaliatory behavior or in an escalation of the original conflict.

Forgiveness does not seek refuge in fairness. Rather forgiveness seeks relief in surrender. Clutching on to pain saps strength and distributes tension throughout the body. Letting go and opening up allows us to relax, to reach out to life and experience the joy of living. Energy wasted to hold back forgiveness and hold in angry feelings can now be put into the service of life-giving and life-fulfilling experiences. Life does not have to be a grim struggle of facing each new day with the distressing reality of one's pain. Facing life with a smile and seeing the world smile back gradually lifts the clouds of unforgiving and lets the light of day shine through.

Forgiveness Is a Better Risk

Each day we take a chance on living. We try to be prepared to maintain control of the circumstances likely to affect our moods and our movements. Although life is not without risks, giving forgiveness a chance is a calculated risk worth taking.

Unforgiving is not as good a risk. It's like having an injury. If you keep the wound open, the abrasive feelings of unforgiving increases the hazards of infection. Even doing nothing hampers healing. You must intervene to restore health, to renew life.

While love is the best health insurance against a diseased heart or distressed soul, it cannot protect us from the destructive forces of living. Evil and misfortune will take their toll regardless of what we do to protect ourselves. But, love can give birth to forgiveness and forgiveness can give birth to resilience, which reduces the risks of dying. Though love may be imperfect, it can improve our chances of being restored to health and help protect us against a further loss of good health. Risking forgiveness is a more cost-effective approach to living. A risk taken is a benefit received; the benefit received is a fuller life of good health.

Forgiving Is Stronger

What we do with our mind affects all aspects of our being, and the mind can be a source of great strength. When we choose with our mind we feel less vulnerable than when we choose with our heart. When we are psychologically hurt, it is our heart that aches; our mind serves up explanations and justifications for the pain. We often conclude that we are victims and want to seek the retribution of revenge. Whether the offending party's behavior is real or imagined, the mind exaggerates the worst motives. We feel what happened was deliberate and unprovoked, cruel and selfish, indefensible and unpardonable.

But, think about this: The same mind that creates the indefensible and unpardonable can also excuse and exonerate. Surely such thinking calls for strength of character and the virtue of mercy. Whose spirit has not genuflected before a person whose mind was able to seek mercy when justice hung in the balance? Who has not struck their own heart in supplication when kneeling before the awe of forgiveness? When the courage of your convictions is grounded in compassion, you are on the path to pardon.

It does take more strength to forgive. We have to work at achieving a verdict wherein benevolence replaces blame and freedom replaces bondage as we are called to an act of mercy. Our feelings of revenge or bitterness are our first defense against further injury; so counteracting these natural tendencies requires the strength to lift the burden of our own grief and the duty-bound guilt we expect from the other party.

Forgiving Fits Faulty People

What we see and hear depends upon the choices we make. Daily we can make growth choices that involve risk or safety choices that protect us against making mistakes. All of our choices depend upon a multitude of factors, especially our willingness to accept ourselves as flawed and vulnerable people. We will experience fright and failure because we are not equipped from birth to meet all the contingencies of living. Yet, our mistakes free us to learn something we could not think, or feel, or do before. While all of our trials will not be triumphs, bridging and bonding can wield small increments of progress into monumental achievements.

Faulty people may also fail to love, but this is only a shortcoming, not a destiny. We can choose our destiny. Instead of always playing it safe and becoming victims of our emotions, we can seek results by using the energy of positive emotions to charge our goals with commitment and infuse our efforts with patience and perseverance. Our faulty ways of looking at the world and our presence in it can be shaped by our optimism and our sense of justice. The pathway to a worthy view of ourselves and a wholesome view of others will become filled with good intentions and pursued with confident consolation.

Injury is also a normal and painful experience of living. We cannot escape injury, physically or psychologically. Instead, we can be awakened to discover the boundless reserves the body has to heal itself. We may have to draw upon these reserves to deepen their powers to heal. Generally we have to touch the wound to assess the damage and dress the hurt. In doing this, we may need to learn how to unburden our hearts so the pain cannot nibble away at our wounds.

Whether the injury is physical or psychological, it is real. The pain does not hide from this identifying experience of living. The forgiveness process helps us locate and identify the injury, extend our hands, and heal our heart. The healing process is one part mystery and one part miracle—both divine ingredients. Together they make injury a distant memory and forgiveness a living bond.

Footnote:

In another <u>Agnes</u> cartoon, she is standing beneath a single outstretched finger of grandma who says, "What do you have to say for yourself, young lady?" Agnes: "Well frankly I did not plan on being caught." She continues her defense in the next panel: "And frankly I prepared no real defense on my behalf. So frankly I think we should just put all this behind us and move on with our lives." The final panel shows Agnes crouched on her bed, hands under her chin and thinking: "Grandmas give very little weight to frankness."

Comment:

Frankly we have said there is no escape from pain when you decide to forgive. Be prepared to be caught trying to avoid it so you can get on with your life. You will be tempted to want to move on and put the painful experience behind you. There is no good defense for avoiding the pain. So you might as well save yourself the trouble.

CHAPTER SIX

Gateway Three: Dealing With the Pain

Making Contact: We generally live between heaven and hell, occasionally knowing the effect and extent of each.

Story: The Monk & The Samurai

ONCE UPON A time, a big, tough samurai went to see a little monk.

"Monk!" he said, in a voice accustomed to instant obedience. "Teach me about heaven and hell!"

The monk looked up at the mighty warrior and replied with utter disdain, "Teach *you* about heaven and hell? I couldn't teach you about anything!"

"You're dirty. You smell bad. You're a total disgrace. Get out of my sight!"

Furious, the samurai drew his sword to slay the monk.

"That is *hell*," the monk said softly.

The warrior was stunned.

He dropped his sword and stared at the monk, and tears of gratitude and peace filled his eyes.

"And that is *heaven*," said the monk.

Comment:

We can cite instances in life when we believe we have had an experience of heaven and hell. We can describe and distinguish between the two and can say something about the impact of each based on our experience. A second-hand account may be useful but the power is in having been in the midst. Although less demonstrative and desirable, we can benefit from being taught by other's experiences of forgiving and being forgiven. We can even help someone speculate and predict what might happen and be accomplished by deciding to initiate or respond to efforts to meet the past and put it behind him/her. Then "to heaven or hell" is seldom a pure experience of either. At times we will get dirty, smell bad, and look unsightly. Occasionally we will look like a rose, smell like a rose, and be a sight to behold. Most likely we will be taught something we could not have learned without drawing our sword, dropping our defenses, and standing defenseless against ourselves definitely softened by and grateful for the experience.

Mark cheated on his wife, Holly. Jenny's best friend, Terry, betrayed her secret. Stacy's uncle sexually abused her. A classmate regularly bullied Sam. These individuals and others have been hurt very deeply and unfairly. They are struggling to cope with the aftermath of these painful situations. How can such individuals deal with their pain in a way that would contribute to their overall emotional well-being? A first step is recognizing the need to enter a process of gradual healing. Selecting appropriate strategies to deal with the pain can start this process.

Most, if not all people do not automatically choose forgiveness as a viable option to resolving pain. In fact, we are often perplexed about the ways to deal with the hurts we experience. We generally begin by considering the particulars of the injury—how, when, and why it happened, how we reacted to it then, and how we are reacting now.

We bring our past and present into our choice of strategy for healing our pain. From the past, we mobilize the method(s) that we may successfully have used to deal with unfair and deep injuries. Our parents, relatives, friends, or heroes may have modeled these strategies for us. From the present, we may bring a blend of emotions and thoughts that help us sort through the possibilities for healing the wounds we believe we do not deserve.

The general approach and specific strategies we decide to use to resolve our pain may not include the person who injured us, regardless of how emotionally close we may be to him/her. That is, we may try our best to heal our wounds without involving the injurer. This strategy is referred to by Enright & The Human Development Group as the intrapersonal strategy to resolving conflict.

Or, we may choose to walk the interpersonal path, which does include the injurer. This path may be chosen for the sake of seeking either justice or mercy. The route we take initially and eventually depends on a number of factors: how much we are hurting, our general style of dealing with conflict, what has worked and not worked for us in the past, our awareness of and need to resolve the pain, and our belief in the effectiveness of the method we select.

The following sections describe intra and interpersonal strategies. Real stories (with fictitious characters) illustrate the essence and particulars of each strategy.

Intrapersonal Path

As you search for options to deal with your pain, you may decide to use, or to avoid using, a resolution approach that excludes the person who injured you. The method you decide on may be positive or negative. You may, for example, decide that putting the hurt and injurer behind you is an appropriate and functional solution. To achieve this objective, you might immerse yourself in pleasurable and comforting activities such as bibliotherapy (reading books to deal with one's emotional upset), physical activity, aesthetic pursuits, or sharing your feelings with someone. Let's look at the merits and shortcomings of these methods.

Bibliotherapy

Using books as a form of therapy is a common way of dealing with emotional hurts. Books let us encounter the journey of others. As we walk their walk, we get in touch with the emotional counterparts and learn other ways to deal with these feelings. We feel less lonely and less vulnerable as we retrace our steps with another. We can explore other destinations and choose another destiny.

One might choose a book that offers a step-by-step formula to deal with a particular problem. Generally, people who select these books want to acquire the skills that have enabled others to triumph over a similar problem. Using such a systematic approach, readers can go at their own pace and gradually acquire, and use skills to deal with a specific problem or similar difficulties.

The potential benefits of this self-focused approach to healing include: the development of positive attitudes and self-image; personal adjustment; relief from emotional tension; the desire to emulate positive experiences of others; and identifying and acquiring of socially appropriate behaviors to deal with personal problems.

However, the choice and quality of books may limit their use as therapy. The relief you seek from the emotional aspects of the problem may be short-lived because you're not dealing with the psychological hold of the injurer. Thus, the transient nature of the catharsis keeps you forever flocking to self-help sections of libraries or bookstores. Although the release of pent-up feelings that books might provide is desirable, it is much more desirable that a person achieve an integration of mind and heart. This integration cannot possibly be achieved through reading alone.

Such integration requires a more active therapy; one that acts out the insights and suggestions gleaned from reading. Without the benefit of trying on new behaviors, the wardrobe hangs in the closet unused. Without trying it on and wearing it in public, you never have a chance to see and experience the wisdom of your selections.

Physical Activity

Linda, a college student, was rejected by her boyfriend and reported that physical activity, such as walking and jogging, kept her mind off her loss and temporarily lessened the heartache she suffered. "I would go jogging to ease my mind every time I felt depressed and sad," she said.

Like many individuals, Linda adopted this strategy to bring about feelings of relief. It has been proven that regular physical exercise such as jogging, walking, swimming, playing tennis, etc. is an antidote to stress and emotional pressure. Again, the emotional release and temporary forgetting that accompanies physical activity does not last very long. Deep feelings of hurt are not subject to escape-oriented activities. In the absence of mediating the activity, thoughts and feelings creep into consciousness and demand your attention. This method, therefore, is not one that can be the sole source of comfort to completely restore our psychological and emotional balance.

Aesthetic Pursuits

After a friend betrayed his secret, Jim turned to aesthetic pursuits to solace his troubled heart. More than ever before, Jim found listening to music, going to concerts, visiting museums, and painting a therapeutic outlet to his deep feelings of hurt. He even subscribed to magazines related to these aesthetic areas of interest.

Interests like these do engage our emotions and draw us into experiences that have lasting effects, because they are the forerunners of habits. Habits become enduring and settled ways of dealing with frequently occurring events. While habits are relatively routine ways of coping, they do counteract tendencies to escape from negative feelings through more passive forms of activity.

Engaging in pleasurable activities, such as the ones Jim chose, is a popular response to the question, "What can I do about my hurt?" These activities substitute enjoyment for distressing feelings and events, while expanding one's cultural horizons. These outcomes are desirable and pose no harm to others or to the person engaged in them. However, the trap is that a person may become so content with the pleasant feelings aesthetic activities provide that he/she may ignore the source of the pain. Like bibliotherapy and physical activity, this strategy provides temporary feelings of relief but fails to address the source of the problem. A temporary escape may develop into a permanent way of evading the problem, robbing the individual of the chance to confront and deal with the heart of the issue.

Negative Methods
Some intrapersonal solutions can reduce the pain but the side effects can be devastating. Some people resort to drugs and alcohol to escape from the pain. Consequently, what begins as a temporary source of relief may end up leading to drug dependence and alcoholism. In addition to the initial hurt, the person also finds him/herself with a drug problem. The potential damage may be incalculable.

In summary, the advantage of using an intrapersonal strategy lies in the temporary relief that it provides. The disadvantage is that the real issue is not dealt with, especially where an escape—albeit negative—is sought. Another shortcoming is the exclusion of the injurer from the resolution process, which may render the process incomplete. Ignoring or avoiding the injurer psychologically makes the injured forever prisoner to the injurer. The aim of resolution must include the injurer if a genuine emancipation from the psychological hold of the injurer is desired.

Interpersonal Strategy
Realizing the temporary relief of the intrapersonal strategy, a person may decide to combine it with tactics that would include the injurer in some way. A person may decide to: talk to someone about the problem; seek justice by taking the injurer to court; take the law into their own hands and mete out punishment; forego punishment; or develop compassion for the injurer.

Talking to Someone
Following their bitter divorce, Nancy spent many hours on the phone and face-to-face talking to her best friend Lisa. Nancy found Lisa's emotional support helped her vent her frustrations and gain a perspective on the situation.

Talking to someone about the injury, especially to a close friend, is a very common interpersonal method used to alleviate pain. We go beyond ourselves to build a social support network. Usually, we begin with people who are close to us, and then move beyond to authority figures such as priests or ministers, superiors at work, or professional helpers. By sharing our feelings with such people, we derive some measure of relief. We also begin to put together a plan of action designed to alleviate problems perpetuating conditions.

A questionnaire containing hypothetical situations of parents doing mean things to their children was given to college students by one author of this book. Many students indicated they chose talking to someone about the issue as a way of dealing with these problems. When asked who that someone would be, a majority of the students said they would talk to a friend and would go see a counselor only if they felt they needed professional help.

The range of people we can talk to—friends, strangers, authority figures, and professional helpers—provide us emotional support, help us understand what we're going through, and suggest ways of dealing with our hurts. They may empathize with us, serve as sounding boards for our feelings and thoughts, and help us cope with our hurts. But, the nature and extent of help that each one offers us depends largely on how well they listen and interpret our problem, and on how accepting and responsive we are to them.

Friends are likely to view and respond to our problem in supportive ways. They listen to us, validate our feelings, cheer us up, and offer ways to deal with our situation. In short, they become our best allies.

Strangers whom we meet by accident in a bus, airplane, or a park might also serve as another outlet for our experience of hurt. Some strangers, especially those who can identify with our concern, will, perhaps, share a similar experience. They may still be grappling with similar emotions and upsets. In so doing, they help us realize that we are not alone in feeling the way we do. They will be a release to some pent up feelings and show us the ways they have chosen to resolve a similar dilemma.

Authority figures, such as religious figures or superiors at work, are often sought out as potentially helpful people. These people look at our concern from a different vantage point. They may take a dispassionate, analytical approach, offering suggestions or helping us devise a plan of action. Their ideas can help us put our concern in perspective and evaluate our readiness to take some action towards resolution.

Professional helpers are another valuable source of support. They actively listen to our concerns, help us discern and clarify our emotions, enable us to take our emotional pulse, and then offer us a process to resolve the source of our distress.

It is clear that talking to someone about our problem is potentially helpful and reassuring. However, a number of possible shortcomings may be involved. For one, the roots of deep and unrelenting hurts might not be dealt with thoroughly. To fulfill their friendship obligations, our friends might find it hard to be objective about the injury and injurer. They might find it especially difficult to tell us if we are irrational or overreacting. We may also grow so dependent on our friends' support that we neglect to tap into our inner resources.

Talking to a stranger sitting next to us in a bus or airplane may only serve the temporary purpose of releasing some pent up feelings. We may feel justified when the stranger expresses a similar concern.

An authority figure may recommend ways of dealing with our hurts, such as reconciling with the injurer and putting the past behind us, which we may not be ready to act upon.

Though desirable and at times necessary, talking to a professional counselor can be both costly and lengthy. It may not be a viable option for everyone. The kind of help the professional counselor can provide may be limited to the known mode of therapy.

All in all, the advantages of talking to someone about our experience, thoughts, and feelings often far outweigh the disadvantages. As a result of talking to someone, we may decide to take a legal action to seek retribution.

Seeking Justice

Going through the legal system is one way to balance the scales of justice by seeking restitution for the wrong done. In the process, however, we may forget that there is an emotional accompaniment to almost every legal claim, feelings that cannot be mitigated by winning a case. Depending on the nature and depth of the hurt, a person who wins a case against the injurer in court may continue to suffer psychologically. This point is illustrated in the following story.

Jim won the custody battle against his wife, Sue, who was having an affair with a workmate and was neglecting and, at times, physically abusing their three children. Although Jim secured custody of the children—a desirable outcome that insured the psychological and physical safety of the children—he still had to heal the wound of his wife's extramarital affairs and her maltreatment of their three children. To resolve the emotional wounds, Jim relied on his own resources—inner strength, the emotional support of relatives and friends, and professional help.

However, some people refuse to use the legal justice system and seek revenge on their own terms. They feel the court system relinquishes their control over the process. Instead they seek retribution or revenge through more direct means. The motto of one seeking vengeance is "a tooth for a tooth," "give them a taste of their own medicine," "revenge is sweet," "get even," "can't let him/her get away with it." Self-righteousness employs retaliatory actions that seem sweet in the short run, but may later result in unfortunate repercussions and/or humbling regrets. The danger in this approach lies in the fact that the injured person defines for himself/herself what measure of punishment is sufficient to even the score. But, emotionally charged thoughts about fairness may culminate in punishments that far exceed the original offense.

One example is the University of Iowa campus shooting by a Chinese graduate student, Gang Lu, in 1992. His actions claimed the lives of two faculty members and an administrator, and brought permanent injury to a student. Gang Lu felt he was dealt an injustice when he did not receive a particular academic award. The meaningless deaths of the victims show how humans set their own standards of justice. Evening the score, no matter how we look at it, can never be achieved by punishment.

Pick up a newspaper any day and you are likely to read an account of a person who has used violent methods to right a wrong in his/her attempt(s) to even the score. The account will often include explanations that defend retaliation as a form of justice.

Are we not supposed to protect and defend ourselves against the injustices of others? By all means, we have to protect and defend ourselves. We must assert our rights and not permit others to violate them. When we are unable to civilly deal with aggressors, cannot settle our disputes or grievances within the legal system, then we must take matters into our own hands. However, when we do, we must be prepared to have the legal system test our claim that justice has been served and weigh our emotional distress in the scales of justice.

There are shortcomings when revenge is motivated by a personal sense of justice. The seeker of revenge finds himself/herself constantly engaged in setting the scales aright. The more hurt the avenger inflicts on the other, the more he/she wants to do it. Thus, revenge adds more fuel to the conflict, endlessly keeping feelings of anger burning.

Offering Mercy

Another avenue an injured person can take is mercy. One can willingly and willfully decide to forego punishing the injurer. In this case, mercy transcends natural aggression and gives life where there once was death. People are drawn together by the common denominator of compassion. The claim to revenge is relinquished in favor of mercy.

This decision is a difficult one for most people to make because, in essence, the person is saying no matter how big the offense, I have love within me sufficient to negate the need. It indeed takes time, effort, energy, courage, wisdom, faith, and hope to reach this point. Giving up one's claim on punishment may be the first step in the pathway to mercy. One can go beyond merely foreswearing resentment and punishment to developing positive feelings, thoughts, and actions toward the injurer.

Here, the injured realizes that the injurer does not deserve the gift of benevolence but nonetheless gives it to him/her freely and unconditionally. Those who have reached this point in their healing journey report they can now begin to wish their injurer well. They cease holding onto ill thoughts, clinging to ill feelings, and contemplating ill actions toward the injurer. They replace the negative thoughts, feelings, and actions with positive ones. In so doing, they experience inner peace and quiet as they celebrate their true freedom from the fetters of resentment, anger, and other negative emotions. Some individuals, especially those whose lives were ruled by anger or hate, report feelings of ecstasy as they bask in the warmth of compassion.

To walk this path, the forgiver must dispel all of the dominant myths about forgiving: that it is impossible to achieve; it is an act of weakness; or it is unwise to do. They have gone against all the odds and courageously worked through their pain and slowly reached the point of psychological release—the endpoint of the forgiveness journey.

Individuals who have gone the mercy route say that in their journey they resorted to short-term strategies such as walking or jogging. In addition, they employed other measures described in this chapter. Each choice was aimed at eradicating the source of their pain. Some who suffered physical ailments, such as asthma or hypertension, as a result of anger or rage report decreased blood pressure and lesser need for asthma medication. On the psychological side, forgivers report a decrease in negative emotions such as anger, resentment, anxiety, and suspicion. Socially, forgivers report that their inner feelings of peace are contagious. They like to be with other people and others enjoy their company.

As far as restoring a previous relationship with the injurer, forgivers must realize the difference between the act of forgiving and the act of reconciling. Forgivers see forgiving as a way to pave the way for reconciliation, knowing that they can decide if reconciling with the injurer is possible or wise. Forgiving is a necessary but not sufficient basis for reconciliation. Sometimes a person may forgive an injurer who is deceased or whose whereabouts are not known, and reconciling with that individual is not possible. While contemplating the notion of reconciling with the injurer, a forgiver must also assess whether it is wise to join the injurer in a relationship again. If the injurer remains unchanged, still abusive, then it is wiser not to reconcile. In such cases, the forgiver must wait in the hope that the injurer will change.

Summary

In summary, when someone hurts us unfairly and profoundly, we invariably search for or employ a way to get rid of the pain. We may initially use indirect ways such as jogging or reading a book that provide us temporary relief. Or, we may try to get rid of our pain by utilizing an interpersonal approach, one that directly includes the person who hurt us. We may do this in one of two ways: by seeking justice or offering mercy. Seeking justice may involve taking the injurer to court or meting out the punishment ourselves.

The other interpersonal route is offering mercy. The act of mercy moves from foreswearing our right to punish the injurer, to developing positive feelings, to accepting of the injurer.

Footnote:

An old farmer had owned a large farm for many years that included a big pond toward the back of the property. When the pond was built, it was properly shaped and fixed up for swimming. The farmer added picnic tables, horseshoe courts, and basketball courts near the pond.

One evening the old farmer decided to check over the pond, as he hadn't been there for a while. As he neared the pond, he heard voices shouting and laughing with glee. When he got closer, he saw a bunch of young women skinny-dipping in his pond. He made the women aware of his presence and they all swam to the deep end of the pond.

One of the women shouted to him, "We're not coming out until you leave!"

The old man replied, "I didn't come down here to watch you ladies swim or make you get out of the pond naked. I only came to feed the alligator."

Comment:

A decision to forgive may involve determining the difference between the bare facts and the naked truth.

And finally…

Five cannibals were hired by a large school district. During the welcoming ceremony the superintendent told them, "You're all part of our team now. You can earn good money here, and you can go to the cafeteria for something to eat. So please, don't trouble any of the other employees." The cannibals promised.

Four weeks later the superintendent returned and said, "You're all working very hard, and I'm very satisfied with all of you. However, one of our janitors has disappeared. Do any of you know what happened to him?" The cannibals all shook their heads "no".

After the boss left, the cannibal leader said to the others, "Which one of you idiots ate the janitor?" A hand raised hesitantly, and the leader replied, "You FOOL! For weeks we've been eating assistant superintendents, curriculum directors, principals, assistant principals, team leaders, supervisors, and coordinators, and no one noticed anything but YOU had to go and eat the janitor!"

We may not notice the results of forgiveness until a merciful person is missing.

CHAPTER SEVEN

Gateway Four: Making the Decision to Forgive

Making Contact: Time to bridge the divide.

Story: The Dog

A DEVOUTLY CHRISTIAN couple felt it important to own an equally Christian pet. After careful inquiry, they went shopping at a kennel specializing in Christian dogs. They found a dog they liked quite a lot. When they asked the dog to fetch the Bible, he did it in a flash. When they instructed him to look up Psalm 23, he complied eagerly, using his paws with dexterity. They were impressed; immediately purchased the animal, and went home (piously, of course).

That night they had friends over. They were so proud of their new Christian dog and his religious skills that they called the dog and began showing him off. The friends were impressed and asked whether the dog was able to do any of the usual dog tricks as well. This stopped the couple cold as they hadn't thought about "normal" tricks. "Well," they said, "let's find out."

Once more they called the dog and they clearly pronounced the command "Heel!"

Quick as a wink, the dog jumped up, put his paw on the guest's forehead, closed his eyes, and began to pray.

Comment:

There are many ways to impress and convince people you have what it takes to be forgiving. You are likely to be most successful if you understand the command to "Heal!" Although you don't need to attend an animal obedience school to learn how to respond to the demand, forgiveness does require knowing about and learning to use the tools that meet the demands of healing. We all want to feel the peace and comfort of being in right relationship with one another. The relationship between a dog and the master is rooted in obedience and faithfulness. Obedience is listening and responding to the voice; faithfulness is listening with an intent to please.

We select the tools to forgive by being obedient to a voice beckoning us to heal. We are the ones who must decide whether to be faithful to our desire to heal. We figuratively crawl up into another's lap, put a hand on their head, and begin to pray. We do not have to purchase anything special to perform upon command but we do have to take command of our inner resources and use them as instruments of healing. Like the doctor who made house calls, we come with our black satchel, put it down, and inquire, "Where does it hurt? What have you already done?," make a diagnoses, and prescribe. We might say, "I believe I know what is causing the pain. This is what we are going to do. What I do will require your cooperation. Together we can make things better." Generally the cure is a combination of medicine and cooperation.

Most acts of forgiving are conditional. The conditions vary from situation to situation, from person to person. Forgiving is as personal and individual as the experience of the original injury. However, the constants are negative thoughts, feelings, and behaviors, (actions) which direct the process.

Why? What Have I Done?

As we look back upon a painful situation, we are bound to ask "why?" Why did this happen to me? What have I done to deserve this? What might have I done to avoid this? Why do I hurt so much? Why should I have to endure this hurt? At first, all of the questions we ask seek relief in explanations. We think the pain will be less pronounced or less severe if reasons can be found for what has happened. Generally, however, we find unacceptable or unsatisfactory answers to our questions. In fact, the answers often contribute to a victim's mentality. "I don't think I have done anything to deserve this," or "I can't understand why someone would do this to me without provocation."

As the answers to the "why" and "what" questions prove unsatisfactory, we begin to seek a remedy in some kind of action. This is part of a total behavior, which is composed of feelings, thoughts, and actions. Feelings prompt the "why" questions and thinking offers explanations for the feelings. But when feelings persist despite explanatory remedies, we begin to look for other ways to deal with the pain. Having unsuccessfully reduced the pain through cognitive explanations (thinking), unconsciously we turn toward the affective (feeling) component to look for a solution. Our feelings engender a number of motives that either promotes a forgiving or an unforgiving posture. Enright (1989) refers to these as styles of forgiveness. These styles of forgiveness are one of several factors that strengthen or weaken our willingness to forgive. Enright's six styles require a progression of responses based on concepts of justice and mercy, and suggest that the individual needs to progress through each stage en route to unconditional forgiveness. For your purposes, each stage will be described and discussed as a motive and as the basis for forgiveness.

Revenge Motive for Forgiveness

Justice is getting even. Retribution is the paramount motive. When an individual cannot repay the wrong by inflicting a hurt, justice is sought through the legal system. The punishment in either case is meant to fit the crime. An eye for an eye mentality drives the forgiveness motive. Getting even involves an exchange of pain. This motive is best satisfied when the party who has been harmed feels the second party has paid the price for their actions. The price is at a minimum equal to the price paid by the revenge seeker. Healing begins when justice has been served.

The revenge motive feels good and seems right. It feels good because your anger has found an outlet. It seems right because no one should inflict pain without suffering similar consequences. However, often the consequences of feeling good and securing retribution have secondary hidden effects. There is always the danger that anger will produce excessively aggressive and exaggerated hostile behaviors, which may create overly severe or irreversible harm and damage. No amount of damage control can rectify the situation.

Even controlled anger and contemplated consequences can be later sources of regret. Every act, whether intended to seek atonement or seek reconciliation, has unforeseen consequences. Often the short-term satisfaction associated with getting even is offset by the long-term misgivings about overreacting or over exacting.

Restitutional or Compensational Motive for Forgiveness

Getting back what was taken, whether a tangible object or an intangible reputation, can be the basis for this type of forgiveness. Recovering what was lost helps re-establish the bond broken by the act. Restitution is accompanied by an expectation of forgiveness. Under these circumstances, you are almost duty-bound to reciprocate by shaking hands and letting bygones be bygones. This expectation is grounded in cultural norms and reinforced by a legal system based upon distributive justice. You are likely to feel guilty if you harbor feelings of ill-will long after appropriate compensation has settled the issue.

However, restitution or compensation can seldom relieve the psychological damage associated with the misery others inflict. While a stolen object might be returned, your ability to trust might be undermined, your feelings of security are jeopardized. You might not be able to let go of hostile and resentful feelings following an apology. Even when words sincerely are expressed, they are mere tokens of regret.

On one hand you want to put the incident behind you, but you also feel cheated if you do. Since the emotional pain is rooted in having lost something, little relief comes when it is recovered. Sometimes what has been lost cannot be regained, and the pain remains as a permanent reminder.

Expectational Motive for Forgiveness

Sometimes the pressure to forgive comes from people close to you who might recognize the harmful effects the unforgiving is having on you. They can view the offending situation or person more dispassionately and remove the emotion that distorts your vision and colors your judgment. They can see more than one way to right the wrong. The need for affiliation is used to exact a forgiveness motive. The squeeze is on and you feel some urgency to fall in line.

But if you aren't ready to forgive, this can create a problem. Readiness often takes time. Psychological units of time differ from those we use to calculate days and weeks. Applying the latter to the former can lead to a serious error in judgment that may compound your emotional turmoil. Then your readiness is actually delayed because you must deal with two types of conflict.

You'll be fighting with yourself and with those close to you. Within yourself, you must come to terms with conflicting motives to forgive and withhold forgiveness. The battle with those close to you is for time and understanding. If you're caught between competing motives, with dissipated emotional energy, you can hardly renew and consolidate your good intentions. And others' good intentions, regardless of how well founded, are no substitute for those you come to as you wrestle with your experience. Pseudo-forgiveness, in response to others' expectations, may bring comfort to others, but it hardly brings solace to you.

Lawful Expectational Forgiveness

Each of us is a member of several social units that express and prescribe expectations as behaviors. Conforming to these expectations defines our status as a member of the group. Expectations order relationships and serve to produce predictable interactions and create group cohesion.

Loyalty to a group's expectations is rewarded with a sense of belongingness and security, knowing we have a group to be with and to count on. However, some degrees of freedom may be relinquished to assume an allegiance to common ideas and ideals. Maintaining and sustaining your membership may create pressures to uphold a high standard of forgiveness.

Standards externally imposed, if not internally endorsed, can create friction among members and tensions within an individual. The reality of a painful experience, inflicted with malicious intent, can make lawful regulation but a pious platitude. When legalities dictate a solution, they can be experienced as harbingers of injustice. They exact a price, the payment of which comes as an exorbitant expense, one often negotiated at an enormous cost to the individual. Group pressure may be temporarily eased to reduce the burden. However, in time the group will insist on some reasonable alignment of group expectations and individual compliance with these expectations. Again, the individual may not be ready to take the high road. However, to choose otherwise is to be left behind. Companionship of the group depends on a shared destination and common routes for getting there.

Forgiveness as Social Harmony

We like closure; we like to settle things, to get things out of the way. But conflict perpetuates a troublesome situation and makes us uneasy. We prefer comfort to discomfort, harmony to discord.

When someone persists in keeping the fires of conflict alive, everyone absorbs part of the heat. The friction that started the fire and the animosity that fuels the flames encroach on other's lives. No one wants to be consumed by the flames of indignation because of a sustained struggle. Once again, social pressure is put on the disputants to yield in the interest of solidarity.

Indecision, even when our peers are willing to withstand prolonged discord, is an unnatural and psychologically draining condition. We may be tempted to settle the dispute just to get relief from the uncertainty. Any solution is better than none. Inner turmoil, spawned by indeterminate haggling and vacillating bouts between guilt and mercy, takes its toll. While there is conflict, there cannot be peace. Coming to the peace table with a proposal to end the strife may be the only way to put an end to the conflict. It may be the form of closure that leaves few stones unturned and fewer of them to throw at one's adversary. Reducing friction in the interest of harmony is in the social interests of society. Without some basis for the mutual resolution of disputes, there can be no basis for the mutual satisfaction of common interests.

Yet peace at any price is not the answer either. Peace purchased without regard to one's resources and one's ability to pay is ludicrous. When real or imagined payments of remorse or surrender are extended over a prolonged time, regrets may begin to renew the conflict and the accompanying feelings.

Peace is a process, rather than a destination. When regrets infiltrate the process, renewed hostility is a likely outcome. The resumption of the conflict may produce even more violent outbursts and many insidious tactics. If you are convinced that the earlier peace accords were flawed and fraudulent, you may keep battling to seek retribution for earlier clashes and compensation for the perceived injustice of the earlier agreement. Thus, the last condition is worse than the first. The battleground has been enlarged and the war is waged on a larger scale. Better to have fought it out to the death earlier than to keep hope alive with a solution hastily conceived and indiscriminately accepted.

Forgiveness as Love

Each of us is known by what we yield. When we harbor evil it eats away at the fruit we bear. All matter of evil, whether it is hatred in its many forms or indifference, creates decay. We cannot store evil in our hearts without bearing the fruit of this evil in our actions. No man or woman can be something he or she is not. For this reason, God always holds out an invitation to goodness, an invitation to bear good fruit. He plants and nourishes the seed that must cultivate in the soil of our hearts. Growth is saying, "yes" to a process. The process takes root in love, bears fruit through faith, and is raised up by hope.

When it comes to forgiving, love begets a process that draws us into faith and hope. Faith is the fruit of a decision to forgive. Hope is the fulfillment of the promise. Indeed, the greatest of these three is love. It is love that bears us up until we can become obedient to the process of conversion inherent in all acts of forgiveness. It is love that draws us back into the unified spirit of humankind. Thus we devote this section to love, the next to faith, and the following one to hope. This trilogy of virtues is the essential feature of a call to conversion as we draw upon these virtues for courage and strength.

Life is a constant call to conversion. We are endlessly challenged to turn away from something and to embrace something else. The challenge is always to become more inclusive, more whole. To be more inclusive is to be open and receptive to that which has been foreign or unacceptable. Love opens the door we have closed behind us. It allows the light of a new day to shine within us and disclose new possibilities. Faith enables us to believe in the possibilities. Hope transforms what might be to what can be. When it comes to forgiveness and to conversion, love first calls us to be a new creation. God is love and as His creation we are called to be lovers.

Love is an act of the will. We can make up our mind to be faithful to ideals that call us up out of ourselves. We can think love. We can choose to be in love. And the more we think it and choose it and pledge ourselves to it, the more obedient we become to a higher power.

To act with fidelity is to become a lover. Believing and becoming are congruent aspects of being: We can be what we want to be. We can become forgivers by first choosing to commit ourselves to the ideals that define what it means to be human and humane.

As we faithfully engage in loving actions, the resistance to forgiveness begins to breakdown. Suppressed desires to let go of the pain are gradually transformed into pain relieving acts of forgiveness. Abandoning the spiteful behaviors releases us from the bondage of ill will and from the shackles of intemperance.

Love enables us to put down our guard. Protecting ourselves with clenched fists and a staunch stance requires an enormous amount of energy but produces little more than a determination to remain unchallenged and unchanged. Remaining in a constant state of readiness, defending ourselves against an inherent inclination to replace evil with goodness also requires a huge investment of energy. How much more sensible it is to invest the energy in behaviors with a potential for paying dividends. Although the yield won't always match the investment, it's better to get some return on the assets of loving than to bury your goodness out of fear of the other party's response.

Yet fear of rejection is an ever-present danger for those who choose to be lovers. The prospect of being a lover is a temptation difficult to resist, yet a temptation one should not resist. We are all looking for love, to receive it and to give it. However, when animosity and acrimony have been constant companions, it is risky to offer the handmaiden of kindness. Weighing the risk puts love to the test of having the will power to let love win the battle.

Although there is always a risk in loving, the gamble is somewhat tempered by our search for the mercy we find in healing relationships. In these relationships, both parties must surrender and let go of their right to be angry, to strike back, or to feel justified. There is a need for conversion if a will to love is involved. Love begins with a conviction that the road to understanding must be paved with more than good intentions. Our good intentions must be reinforced with courage and brought to fruition by forbearance. Based on these commitments, we can begin to build relationships marked by purpose, endurance, and resolve.

The tenets of relationships marked by love include the following:

<u>Love is believing we are all connected to one another and we must strive to maintain these connections.</u>
Unity is the object of forgiveness. Forgiveness is getting in the right relationship with others. But we must be convinced restoring severed connections is important. The electric current of solidarity cannot flow through wires severed by animosity and acrimony. When we pull the plug on love, we soon observe a loss in the vital signs of life. Love seeks to restore what has been lost, to bring light when there was darkness, to bring healing where there has been pain.

Someone has to take the initiative. Someone must remember what it is like to be refused the gift of understanding. Someone must be obedient to creation, to the brotherhood and sisterhood of humankind. Someone must surrender vanity and seek unity. The person of love values the link between God and humankind and looks for ways to include everyone in the circle of God's goodness.

<u>Love is believing in the truth of the holy scripture.</u>
Surrendering to a higher wisdom is a loving response to the holy scripture. Through the holy scripture, we are assured and reassured about the need for and the benefits of forgiveness—to forgive seventy times seven to bring about peace and justice. Yet we persist in holding onto our grudges and exacting a price beyond repair because we seek solace in revenge.

<u>Love is believing in prayer.</u>
We take our anger to God and seek a less destructive outlet. Usually, when we're offended, we seek retribution. We want the other party to suffer. We find it difficult to be faithful to a forgiveness that seeks conversion rather than compensation. Prayer can be a conversion experience when we allow it to become a guiding force in our lives. Prayer breaks down resistance. Like all conversations with those we love, it opens the doorway to our hearts and allows others to cross the threshold of our good intentions. A conversation that begins with God will eventually be enlarged to encircle the object of our resentment. As we listen, we begin to see in ourselves the possibilities hidden by our staunch desire to get even. Through faithful listening, we begin to understand our inner need to be at one with ourselves and with others. It is difficult to resist the call to be centered in God and in the gifts of His creation.

Prayer provides us with corrective lenses to see more clearly when it comes to forgiveness. We look with a new sense of reality and as visionaries with a mission. Prayer calls us out of our blindness into the light of each new day.

Prayer connects us to the One who can absorb our anger and exchange it for peace. God can transform the energy that seeks to inflict to an energy that seeks harmony. Love leads us to use prayer to refocus our thoughts and redirect our energy. Energy born out of conflict can be reborn as conciliation.

<u>Love can mediate in our efforts to reconcile our motives of fairness and justice.</u>
Life is not fair. Certainly it seems most unfair when we assume greater responsibility for the origins and consequences of conflict. We feel put off and put out by thoughts of going the extra mile to make amends. "Why should

I be so much more concerned or be so much more responsible for making a wrong right? Why should I appear to absorb a disproportionate amount of the blame/fault for situation?" These are standard questions and reasonable reactions. Yet they assume elements of fairness can be weighed and equally distributed in the scales of justice.

The person with a will to love will be less concerned with whom than with what. Rather than being troubled by who did what, we become troubled by what can be done. Asking what can be done is a healthy way to acknowledge that fairness is merely an abstraction. Solutions are found in imagination and good will. It matters not how much, but how little can I expect and still get us back together.

<u>Love is a blessing, a gift of the presence of God that must be shared</u>.
Those blessed with the gift of love know who they are and whom they can be. They live each day accepting one part of themselves while stretching for the other. Believing in themselves they find it easier to believe in others. Aware of their potential for good, they seek it faithfully. Remaining centered in this blessing enables them to remain centered in the One who is the origin of all blessings. Properly centered, they can reach out in many directions and draw others into the blessings as well.

Being forgiving is learning how to be present to others, even when it occasionally means denying and defying ourselves. Self-denial does not mean sacrificing yourself, but rather sacrificing your right to be right about the things that matter little. Saving face matters little when we are called to be the face of God.

<u>Finally, love is a readiness to act</u>.
When we choose love as a life principle, we prepare ourselves to enter into the spirit of forgiveness. Love does not wait for the other party to come around. Persons who do that remain unmoved by efforts to reconcile, for to do so would demand something they are unprepared to do. Becoming a giver, and taking little in return, creates a surplus of love that we need to understand relationships torn by the strife of deficit loving.

Readiness to act begins with a willingness to admit wrongdoing and to acknowledge grievances. Love is daring to be honest with yourself and with the offending party. But it is also daring enough to look for common ground. Where there is division there is little chance for understanding. When we are captive to our differences we are not free to see our common strivings. Love helps forge the optimism and reassurance that we can find common ground.

Conclusion

Love is the first step in the process of conversion. Without love we cannot begin to believe our way into unnatural ways of acting. Love is a firm conviction that we can make a difference. Love is trusting God and trusting you to be sufficient to the demands of the task. Taking a stand for forgiveness, refusing to back down in the face of adversity, and working to achieve unity are not the choices of those with little faith.

Love makes faith a habit. Love is the surest way to enter life as a forgiver and to forge the tools of forgiveness. Habits are enduring ways of thinking about and doing life. Habits operate almost automatically and out of awareness. They do not seek explanations and justifications. They operate as though the best way has been found. Why trouble yourself with other's possibilities? When love fashions a faith that becomes a habit, we are more likely to trust others and to trust ourselves. We are more likely to believe we all seek the same thing—a secure place in one another's heart.

Footnote:

A man was struck by a bus on a busy street. As he lay near death on the sidewalk, a crowd of spectators gathered around.

"A priest. Somebody get me a priest!" the man gasped.

A policeman checked the crowd and yelled, "Is anyone a priest?"

Out of the crowd stepped a little Jewish man at least 80 years old.

"Mr. Policeman," said the man, "I'm not a preacher. I'm not even a Christian. But for 50 years now I'm living behind the Catholic church on

First Avenue, and every night I'm overhearing their services. I can recall a lot of it, and maybe I can be of some comfort to this man."

The policeman agreed and cleared the crowd so the man could get through to the injured man.

The Jewish man knelt down, leaned over the injured man, and said in a solemn voice, "B-4, I-19, N-38, G-54, O-72…"

Comment: Doing Our Best in an Emergency

We cannot always pick the time and the place to reconcile our differences. Sometimes we live at the edge of a single chance to make things right. Someone may come along to help us who is well-intentioned but may be ill-prepared. However, in an emergency it is not the substance but the spirit of the situation that matters. Is this just the loving thing to do?

CHAPTER EIGHT

Gateways Five & Six: Forgiveness Tools

Making Contact: Getting the job done does require skill and use of the right tools.

Story:

A MAN WAS walking in the city when he was accosted by a particularly dirty, shabby-looking bum who asked him for a couple of dollars for dinner. The man took out his wallet, extracted two dollars and asked, "If I give you this money, will you take it and buy whiskey?"

"No, I stopped drinking years ago," the bum said.

"Will you use it to gamble?"

"I don't gamble. I need everything I can get just to stay alive."

"Will you spend the money on greens fees at a golf course?"

"Are you MAD? I haven't played golf in 20 years!"

The man said, "Well, I'm not going to give you two dollars. Instead, I'm going to take you to my home for a terrific dinner cooked by my wife."

"Won't your wife be furious with you for doing that? I know I'm dirty, and I probably smell pretty bad."

The man replied, "Hey, man, that's OK! I just want her to see what a man looks like who's given up drinking, gambling, and golf!"

Comment:

Sometimes it is a matter of selecting the right tool when you want to get the job done. You may have to stop drinking at the well of self-pity. You may have to spend some time deciding what you will do. Forgiveness is not intended to be a gamble, although it is also not a sure thing. It's kind of like golf, swing away! You may not make par the first time around the course, but, if you practice, you may surprise yourself with an occasional drive straight down the fairway, an approach shot that lands on the green, or a putt that deftly makes its way to the cup. You may not look like a man who wants to impress his wife, but it is better than being content with a couple of bucks.

At this point of your forgiveness journey, you have made a tentative commitment to use forgiveness as a means to healing your pain, and possibly to restore a broken relationship. This commitment gradually softens your heart, and eases your mind. As this occurs, you become more willing to actively engage in strategies that would eventually set you free from pain.

In this chapter, you will learn six strategies, or tools of forgiveness, to use in the process of forgiving. A section devoted to each strategy includes a definition of the strategy, the factors that hinder or facilitate it, and cautions about using of the strategy.

Let's begin with a brief overview of each strategy. Reframing, or reattribution, involves seeing your injurer and the injury from a new perspective (Gateway Five) This strategy will be stressed more than the others (Described in Gateway Six) because of its pivotal influence on the forgiveness process as well as its facilitative impact on the rest of the strategies. Developing empathy (feeling how the injurer feels) and developing sympathy (suffering with the other) are two additional tools. Accepting your pain without harboring it is a fourth strategy, which, in the end, brings release. The fifth strategy requires recognizing that you have needed forgiveness from someone in the past. The sixth strategy deals with accepting the permanent change in you due to the injury.

Gateway Five: Reframing

Reframing can be used to strengthen and enact your commitment to forgiving the person who injured you. This strategy is based on the premise that human beings do not inflict pain for the sheer sake of creating pain for others. Rather, we inflict pain as a way of dealing with, or compensating for, our own suffering.

To reframe, we first assemble information to understand the causes of our own and other people's behaviors. This may include recollections that may be influenced by the time that has passed since the transgression. However, accuracy as objective fact is less important than understanding situations that have perpetuated feelings of unforgiving. The explanations or judgments that we finally arrive at generally lead to conclusions about the motives of the other party. We ask ourselves, "Why did this person treat me this way? Whatever possessed him/her to engage in this hurtful behavior?" Generally, we conclude the motives are rather stable, predictable personality characteristics, or relatively stable and unstable situational factors. In either case, we may decide the person has less control over his/her actions because they are well-ingrained personal inclinations or habitual ways of responding to conflict. Understanding this we become more disposed toward forgiveness. We begin to talk to ourselves differently about the injurer.

The explanations or attributions we construct have powerful effects on our feelings, plans, moods, hopes, and well-being. At times, when these effects not only create tension and stress, but also can be psychiatrically dangerous ways of coping. In such cases, reframing, or reattribution, can be of great benefit. In reframing, you reinterpret both the injurer's qualities and the injury itself by viewing them in a new context shaped by an appraisal of motives, external pressures, and the injurer's history. Against this backdrop, you reframe or reappraise what happened and allow yourself to see aspects of the injurer that you were previously unable or unwilling to see. The purpose behind your reexamination, however, is not to downplay the hurt (this would be condonation, not forgiveness), but to begin to view the other in a larger context.

Steps of Reframing

The first step is to challenge and examine our assumptions about the personal forces, which influenced the injurer's disposition. A battered woman, for example, may make the following dispositional attribution about her battering husband, "He has a violent temper which causes him to batter me," a personal characteristic that is stable and may not be subject to much change. To attribute the causes to a situation, the battered wife might focus on the fact that her husband is unemployed. This situation is unstable and subject to change.

The second step is to make attributions about aspects of the injurer's intent. As in the first step, we attempt to distinguish between intrinsic and extrinsic factors. Again, the battered woman may make an attribution related to intentionality, "He deliberately meant to inflict harm," or responsibility, "I deserve it." These attributions may lead to undeserved self-blame or counterproductive accusations of the other. It would be healthier to focus on aspects in the injurer's history to understand the injurer as the composite of experience that shape the way he thinks. His or her past history may have been punctuated by episodes of parental physical abuse.

A third step is to separate the injurer from the injury to really "see" the truth about the injurer. He/she is a weak, needy, and fallible human being. This assessment, free of negative emotions like hate and resentment, may reveal more of the "real" truth about our injurer.

Factors that Influence Reframing

Attributions that open the door to forgiveness are not likely to immediately follow the injury. When a person injures us, two factors determine how quickly or how slowly we forgive the injurer. The first is related to the sense we make out of the injury: (a) how "reasonable" the person appears to be, (b) whether his/her actions are intentional, and, if intentional (c) who is at fault. Fault may be attributed to personality or to external factors that motivate the person. The attributions we make partly determine whether we decide to retaliate, forgive, avoid the injurer, or pursue some other course of action.

The second factor deals with the notoriously biased nature of the attributions human beings make. Our strategy to resolve conflict may be based on inaccurate or exaggerated explanations of the other person's behaviors. Therefore, attributions may contribute to our decision to grant or withhold forgiveness. When withheld, we suffer in more than one of the following ways for our erroneous or dysfunctional attributions: from depression and anxiety caused by an unfavorable view of the self (e.g., seeing oneself as an unlikable person); from hate, resentment, and anger toward the other; from an exacerbation of the very symptoms that gave rise to the attribution; from an increasing distance and sense of difference from others; from an inability to forgive the other.

To help prevent individuals from suffering such adverse effects of negative attributions, the action of reframing is worthwhile to initiate the process of forgiving.

Cautions in Use of Reframing

As you begin reframing, remember that it does not occur in one single act but occurs slowly. The deeper the injury is, the more difficult and slower the reframing process evolves. Regardless of the case, the new perspective you develop of the injurer is usually achieved by your genuine attempts to understand the injurer's ways of thinking and believing. As this occurs, you will gain the growing awareness that the injurer's behavior may very well be attributed to his/her way of perceiving the world or prior hurtful events. In cases where the injurer is a significant other, you may gradually realize that the person has loved as much as he/she was capable of loving. Believing he is unloved or incapable of loving, he might not be able to give what he hasn't been given or learned to give.

The more positive and genuine the reframing is, the more able you will be to forgive. This fact is supported by the personal testimony of a man named Kiel who used reframing to forgive the person who shot him and caused his paralysis from the waist down. Kiel put his new perspective of his injurer, a perspective that grew out of compassion, in these words, "I forced myself to pray for that man. As I did, a degree of compassion for him grew within me. Though I was severely handicapped, I had God to lean upon. The man who shot me probably did not. My attitude began to improve" (p.13).

Smedes in his 1984 book, Forgive and Forget: Healing the Wounds We Don't Deserve, aptly underscores the therapeutic nature of positive attributions:

When you forgive someone for hurting you, you perform spiritual surgery inside your soul; you cut away the wrong that was done to you so that you can see your "enemy" through the magic eyes that can heal your soul. Detach the person from the hurt and let it go, the way a child opens his hands and lets a trapped butterfly go free. (p. 27)

Gateway Six: Additional Forgiveness Tools
Empathy

Empathy is a second strategy that we can use to forgive another person. In this process we attempt to understand another person's feelings and thoughts. We reach out for the person who injured us to get to know him/her more. When we empathize, we try 'to put ourselves in that person's shoes.' Carl Rogers, the noted psychologist, wrote that empathy involves "entering the private perceptual world of the other person, temporarily living in that person's life, and moving around within it nonjudgmentally, delicately, and sensitive to the felt meanings and values of that person, and also being sure to check and communicate with the person as you go" (p. 4). This description clearly indicates that to empathize we must adopt the other person's psychological viewpoint, or, what some call "fellow-feeling."

Steps of Empathy

Empathy can be used to gather data about the injurer and clarify the problem. It involves an awareness of the influence of feelings upon the thoughts and actions of someone else. As you attempt to adopt your injurer's affective viewpoint, you'll find three steps need to be followed. First, you need to be able and willing to detect the various emotions your injurer must have been experiencing before, during, and after inflicting the injury on you. After detecting feelings, you try to see what experiences or circumstances might account for the injurer's feelings. Second, you need to have the capacity and the willingness to adopt your injurer's perspective to experience his or her emotional state. And third, you need to be aware of the complementary feelings aroused within you as you engage in this process.

Cautions in the Use of Empathy

As you engage in the strategy of empathy, remember that your empathic involvement must be genuine and sensitive. You must be willing to enter your injurer's way of seeing the world to understand his or her feelings and thoughts. You must be able to enter into their feelings and thoughts without being judgmental. In other words, you must resist labeling the thoughts and feelings whether they are good or bad, desirable or undesirable.

Pseudo empathy might lead you to condone what the injurer did to you. This caution is related to your emotional reactions to the injurer. If you still feel angry or resentful toward the injurer as you try to empathize, try to work through your anger first. Your anger may interfere with your ability to sensitively and accurately feel what your injurer is feeling.

In conclusion, empathy can be a powerful tool to understand as objectively as possible the emotional life of the person and how feelings contribute to decisions, choices, and ways of expressing. The goal of empathy is not to condone or excuse the injurer from what he or she did. Empathy and how to empathize are eloquently described in the following quote:

> *To care for another person, I must be able to understand him and his world as if I see it. I must be able to see, as it were, with his eyes what his world is like to him and how he sees himself. Instead of merely looking at him in a detached way from the outside, as if he were a specimen, I must be able to be with him in his world, "going" into his world in order to sense from <u>"inside" what life is like for him, what he is striving to be and what he requires to grow.</u>*

Sympathy

Sympathy is derived from the Greek word "sympatheia"—sym means "with" and pascho means, "to suffer." Based on this, sympathy means to suffer with another person whose suffering can be undertaken in the context of our own. The sameness can be attributed to our human condition and our affinity to experience much of life in similar ways. This affinity based on our feelings serves at least two purposes: (1) it provides us with clues as to the feelings of the other person; and (2) it creates in us a willingness to consider ways to alleviate their pain as we deal with our own.

This definition comprises the cognitive component, which includes an acknowledgement of the other person's pain, and the conative, which is manifested in our altruistic desire to abate the other person's pain.

Steps of Sympathy

To engage in sympathy, you need to first know the demands this strategy places on you. You must be both ready and willing to acknowledge your injurer's pain. You may ask, "Why in the world would I want to acknowledge my injurer's pain? After all, he or she was the one who caused me all this pain?" These are realistic and reasonable questions, and good answers must be given before you can be motivated to understand the suffering of your injurer. Understanding can provide clues into the emotional and psychological world of your injurer. You may discover that your injurer might have behaved similarly given similar circumstances. Understanding the negative life events that precipitated the behavior might help you feel less offended or retaliatory.

As you become more inclined to sympathize with your injurer, check your emotions and be sure they won't stand in your way of understanding the feelings of your injurer. You must be able to believe the other person acted without being fully in command of his/her emotions and is now experiencing some regret for his/her actions. While not condoning those actions, you are not holding the person totally responsible. Remember, you cannot genuinely countenance the actions of your injurer without dealing with the negative emotions these actions have evoked in you. In the absence of these conditions, it is difficult to feel charitable toward this individual.

Finally, before we sympathize with another individual, we need to understand our motivation for doing so. We seek consolation by recalling our own fallibility, our own imperfections in the face of trying situations. We all make regrettable mistakes. Surely the other person has regrets. The pain is a mutual experience of our shortcomings as human beings. Being concerned about the well-being of a fellow human being ennobles all of humanity. If we do not help, hurt becomes a way of life.

Cautions in the Use of Sympathy

We must first distinguish between our own feelings and those of the other person. As we seek understanding, it may be sufficient to acquiesce, to gently dismiss our claim for retribution. We may choose not to take an action to alleviate the pain of the sufferer as we try to get rid of our own pain.

Secondly, when we sympathize, we more or less exchange places with the other person. In doing this, we may misconstrue the way the other person perceives the event. We may excuse them because we think they see it as we do. We may mistakenly believe they harbor regrets. However, they may not share our pain or feel the least bit responsible for it. Part of the difficulty deals with the complexity of human motives and the idiosyncratic expression of them. In addition, people have different action thresholds—some are impulsive while others are reflective. That is, some people don't act as responsibly as others.

In addition, sharing responsibility for another person's actions or excusing them because of similar shortcomings in awareness requires emotional strength. Although, kindness and compassion do not come easily, emotional readiness is a prerequisite to sympathy.

Finally, keep in mind not to confuse sympathy with empathy. In empathy, the self is the vehicle for experiencing the life of another. In sympathy, our concern is to achieve communion with another. When we empathize, we substitute ourselves for the other person; when we sympathize, we substitute others for self. The goal of empathy is for us to know what something would be like for the other person; the aim of sympathy is for us to know what it would be like to be that person. Furthermore, in empathy we act "as if" we were the other person, while in sympathy we are the other person. As we empathize, we seek awareness, and as we sympathize, we seek understanding. In sum, empathy is a way of experiencing, while sympathy is a way of relating.

Assimilating the Pain

Assimilating or absorbing the pain we experience following the initial injury is, indeed, a paradoxical tool of forgiveness—To get rid of the pain we are feeling, we need to take it into ourselves. Like metabolizing food, it must be absorbed and dispersed throughout the system. A change takes place as pain participates in the process of forgiveness. This act is a willful and conscious one in which we courageously let go of all the factors (such as psychological defense mechanisms of denial and repression) that bind us to the pain. Our act of pain absorption is a testimony that we were hurt and suffered in many ways. In addition, our willingness to absorb the pain at this point in our forgiveness journey speaks of our readiness to abandon the maladaptive ways we have employed to cope with the pain, such as denying what happened. We proclaim: No more denial, repression, or blame. We face what happened head on. The following section shows how.

Steps to Assimilating the Pain

As with the previous tools of forgiveness, specific steps can be followed to accept the pain.

1. You must first admit that some harm or damage has been done, that you have been physically or psychologically wounded. You are very aware of the form of damage, who did the damage, and the period over which the damage was done. Consider John and Jody, parent survivors of an adolescent suicide victim, who must accept the fact that their son, Rick, did commit suicide by hanging himself in the back yard of their house after breaking up with his girlfriend. The damage has been done. There is no way to undo it. Denial behaviors

that Jody used as a defense against the acceptance of the pain now need to stop. She cannot go to Rick's bedroom to kiss him good night, or tell her husband, John, that she just gave Rick a kiss good night. She needs to come to terms with Rick's suicidal death, that Rick is no longer among the living. She can no longer protect herself against this reality. Although this is very difficult to do, accepting the fact that Rick is gone is much more liberating than hanging onto an unalterable fact of life.

2. Next, we must admit that we experienced the hurt. We are "damaged goods." We have to recover from the assault on our well-being. We begin to accept our emotional reaction to the injury as something natural, and not something to be ashamed of or to incapacitate us. We acknowledge that as human beings we felt anger, resentment, guilt, anxiety, sadness, betrayal, or shame. We no longer have to manufacture defense mechanisms to distance ourselves from the pain. Now, we must find ways to demolish the deceptive psychological processes that separated us from our pain.

3. Next comes the realization that one possible way of dealing with such pain is to absorb or accept it as a natural consequence of the injury. This act of acceptance is done willfully and willingly.

Precautions in the Process of Assimilating the Pain (Damage Control)

As you become convinced that accepting the pain is a way of freeing yourself of the original hurt, keep the following precautions in mind as you accommodate yourself to the hostilities, which precipitated the event. The differences may still remain but you are now trying to settle into a life, which acknowledges them without accepting the way they were expressed. Be aware that:

Assimilating the pain is not synonymous with condoning what happened. You still hold the other person responsible for what he/she did, and you wholeheartedly do not think or believe that the pain the other person caused you did not matter.

Assimilating the pain does not mean submissive surrender to the pain and to the injurer. On the contrary, this act is conscious, courageous, and, if anything, it is a triumphant way to say: "I no longer allow myself to submit to the need to get even."

Assimilating the pain must be genuinely felt in every particle of your existence. It should stem from the depth of your heart and mind.

Assimilating the pain means that the decision to do so is not done in a fleeting moment lacking in alertness, but rather the decision is a deliberate act and one that has been contemplated for a while.

Assimilating the pain does not mean reliving the hurt. You have worked through much of your negative emotion when you reach this final station of forgiveness. It does not mean you no longer experience intense negative reactions toward your injurer. Hurt can only be absorbed after it has been worked through. If not, swallowing the pain is bound to cause a nauseating case of psychological indigestion.

In summary, accepting the pain is a conscious, daring, and vital step on your journey to forgiveness. By accepting the pain, you admit that you were hurt, and you suffered undue pain as a result. Your effort at absorbing the pain is buttressed by the hope that the pain you assimilate will set you free. This sense of freedom is characterized by a cohesive sense of self. The self is now in a state of balance or integration compared to its previous state of fragmentation. You begin to enjoy inner peace and quiet as you become enveloped by an overall sense of emotional stability and well-being.

In a sense, the experience of pain assimilation and accommodation that brought about the inner state of equilibrium elevates you to a higher level of personhood. The assimilated pain has made you a stronger and healthier human being through a growth-producing opportunity. With your sense of humanity restored, you begin to look beyond yourself. More opportunities for growth and self-discovery lie ahead. You are no longer preoccupied with yourself; you look beyond yourself to others who are hurting and to those whom you may have hurt in the past. You discover the need to be forgiven by those whom you hurt in the past, acknowledging the fact that you have been changed, perhaps permanently, by the hurt. The importance of this self-discovery is discussed in the next two sections.

Realization: Acknowledging Our Need for Forgiveness

All of us have flaws or faults. We have inflicted our own damage over the years, while others have been our victims. This realization of our own shortcomings, knowing we have unfairly and deeply hurt someone in the past and that we desired to be forgiven, can serve as a powerful, motivating factor to forgive the person who hurt us. We know what it feels like to be resented, reproofed, and alienated by the person we hurt. We are more keenly sensitive to the full range of feelings our injurer may be experiencing and can now more fully comprehend that person's desire for recompense. We are now able to garner feelings of remorse or guilt and muster the desire to restore the broken relationship. Several steps can help do this effectively.

Steps to Self-Realization of Forgiveness

1. You must be able to isolate the incident in which you were the injurer and recall your feelings and thoughts immediately after the incident and thereafter. The more affect you can arouse, the more likely you are to understand the emotions your injurer might be experiencing.
2. Reflect on what motivated you or influenced you to do what you did. Did you intend to hurt that person? If so, why? If not, what accounts for the ill will between you? Did you feel differently about what you did sometime later? What steps did you take, if any, to share these feelings with the person whom you hurt? How did that person react to your efforts to reconcile? Answering these questions might help you view hurtful behavior as intentional or unintentional. Intent becomes an important factor in both your readiness to forgive and in what you consider as appropriate ways to reestablish the relationship. We are generally more willing to forgive inadvertent or unintentional hurtful acts.

Cautions in Using Self-Realization as the Basis for Forgiveness

As you acknowledge your own need for forgiveness, dwell on the following considerations:

1. It is important not to feel compelled to forgive the person who hurt you just to see yourself as a forgiving person. Guilt associated with being unforgiving may be a good basis for reviewing the incident and questioning your own part in it, but guilt should not be the primary motive for acting forgivingly. Love may be absent from guilt, and ultimately forgiveness is an act of love.
2. It is crucial to know that your feelings after hurting someone may be very unlike those of the person who hurt you. You may have felt remorseful and wanted to apologize and restore the relationship. The person who hurt you may not have had these feelings at all. It is vitally important to base your forgiveness of the person on how you feel toward him or her, rather than on how he or she felt or is feeling toward you.
3. Guard against self-righteousness. You will continue to harbor feelings of ill will toward the other person if moral justification is an attitude of virtuousness or is a primary motive. Neither justice nor harmony is served when you forgive someone because you want to absolve the other party from feelings of guilt, remorse, or shame. It is quite possible that the person who hurt you may have forgotten about the incident or just does not think it warrants much attention. This attitude is likely to become strikingly apparent when you extend the hand of friendship.
4. Avoid making any assessment of your injurer's present behaviors toward you. If you become preoccupied with questions such as: Is that person remorseful, guilty, or does he/she acknowledge what has been done to me? You are unwittingly placing a condition on your forgiveness. Forgiveness is not contingent on that person showing remorse, sorrow, or guilt. Otherwise, that person dictates the terms of forgiveness. You lose the initiative to do what you decided best expresses your coming to terms with this situation.

It is a wonderful feeling to finally be in a position where you are sufficiently free to reflect on the impact of your past behaviors on others. It is healthy to acknowledge your past in situations requiring forgiveness. You, too, have been the guilty party. The guilt was awful. Now in the forgiver position, insight and compassion become tools for fueling your desire to forgive the other person. The act of forgiveness sets two human souls free; your own and that of the person who wronged us. This is an ultimate act of wisdom, altruism, and good will.

Acceptance as a Change in Identity

With the assimilation of pain, we become more willing to accept the fact that the offense against us may have resulted in a permanent change in our sense of self (identity). This change in the way we define and view ourselves may be physical or psychological. Having been deformed or paralyzed after being shot by someone would affect one's sense of physical well-being. The change may be psychological—becoming more cautious, being less likely to trust—after having been betrayed. An example of a permanent change in physical self, and even psychological self, is illustrated by Kiel's (1986) personal journey of forgiveness. Kiel was shot by someone and as a result was paralyzed from the neck down. His inability to walk, being confined to a wheel chair, limited his activities. He became more dependent on others, less free to schedule his activities. His sense of deformity and self-reliance were jeopardized.

Another example of a permanent physical and psychological change is a female incest survivor. She is no longer a virgin; she has been violated. Bitterness, or even self-loathing, may undermine her ability to deal with people.

Steps to Identifying Changes in Self

The following are steps will help you identify permanent changes in yourself as a result of the hurt you experienced.

1. First, know exactly what the nature of the hurt was. Was it physical, psychological, emotional, or moral?

2. Make an overall assessment of how you were before the hurt and how you are after the hurt. Compare the two conditions. What change or changes took place in your view of yourself and/or in the way you conduct your affairs? What impact has the experience had on your view of life or your approaches to relationships in general?
3. After assessing the nature and extent of change, examine the particulars of change. If the change is in trusting others, your task is to find out whether you have now become less trusting of certain individuals and under certain situations. Or, is this a pervasive condition, which contributes to wariness in all situations? In other words, look at specific ramifications of the change.
4. Following comes the issue of the adequacy and reasonableness of the adaptations that must and need to be made to function better in life. For example, it was necessary for Kiel to use the wheelchair to get around. Kiel would have to positively adjust to mobility problems and to people's attitudes toward the disabled. The point here is to do the best you can with the after effects, if any, that the hurt precipitated.

Precautions in Dealing with Identity Changes

It is one thing to realize that someone hurt us, and it is another to realize and accept that hurt resulted in a lasting change in ourselves. Several cautions are advisable as you adjust to the change in your sense of self, following the injury. Here are some to ponder:

1. Some changes, especially physical injuries, may cause conspicuous deformities that alter the way you look at yourself and at how others look at you. Gauge your feelings toward the disfigurement or the physical impediment. It is especially important to guard against negative self-views that can gradually lead to feelings of lessened self-esteem.
2. As you accept the change in your perceptions of who you are and who you are in relation to others, we must also guard against the inclination to use the physical or psychological scars as constant reminders

of the injustice done to you. Visible scars, such as burns on the face, may strengthen feelings of self-other comparisons, especially in an appearance-conscious society. Such comparisons may lead to feelings of low self-worth or arouse unfavorable emotions toward the injurer.

3. The more the change in you is permanent, the more difficult it is to accept. Therefore, expect this process to be slow and gradual. It will take some time before you can feel inwardly comfortable with the change in your identity.
4. As with the previous tools of forgiveness, you must guard against pseudo-acceptance of change in yourself. The feelings ought to be real; otherwise you may end up with contradictory feelings that could torment you.

In summary, identifying and accepting change incurred by the hurt is an important part of the forgiveness process. Some changes are easier to know, accept, and adjust to than others. The process does take time. In many respects, it serves as an ultimate test of our forgiveness. Integrating the changes has an enduring effect on the way we see ourselves and the way we lead our lives. In our attempts to integrate the change, we may experience a resurgence of negative emotions toward the injurer. This indicates that we have more work to do. If we don't feel negative emotions, then we have made positive progress toward emotional health and psychological freedom.

Each tool of forgiveness contributes something to the repair of a relationship. When used in combination, these strategies enable us to construct a new basis for understanding.

We first examined reframing, which simply means seeing the person who hurt us in a different light. Seeing ourselves differently is the last of the six tools, and involves our accepting a change in our identity. Each phase of our forgiveness journey gradually frees us from pain and demands a serious and honest reading of our emotional temperature. We often run hot and cold when it comes to issues of forgiveness. However, our emotional health depends upon our willingness to use the tools and to handle any unresolved issues encountered along the way.

The forgiveness tools require steadfast patience and endurance. The process of resolving pain may be agonizingly slow at times. Don't get discouraged. Continue to be undaunted in your efforts toward self-discernment and self-change. Forgiveness tools are only as good as the hands of those who use them. Being handy is as much an attitude as an aptitude. You must want to rebuild a relationship or reconstruct your life. Properly used, these tools of forgiving can transform you from the angry, fearful, resentful individual into a tolerant, understanding, happy, and loving person. Only you can control the direction and extent of change.

The personal stories in this chapter, which were shared by people who used the forgiveness tools, show that their lives without forgiveness were ones of bondage. Their worlds were dominated by powerful negative emotions. The urge for revenge was always pulsating through them. But with forgiveness, their lives became enriched, empowered, and free. The act of forgiving made them better, stronger, and more understanding of themselves and others.

In addition to renewing their faith and restoring their love, forgiveness has rekindled their sense of hope. Instead of being locked into a mentality of bitterness, forgiveness has given them a new lease on life. They can face the world and themselves with a greater sense of self-assurance and self-realization. Those who plant a seed and care for its growth reap the fruits of forgiveness.

Footnote:

I am looking at a 3-panel <u>Agnes</u> comic strip devoted to a science homework assignment. In the first panel, Agnes addresses her grandma, "I need beakers! I need test tubes! I need huge heaps of pseudo-scientific paraphernalia!!" She adds in the second panel, "I will strew them around and distract the judges from the insanity of my project." To that her grandma replies, " I have some butter tubs in the refrigerator, but I'm not going to just dump them out." Agnes responds in the final panel, "I doubt Jonas Salk had to choke down old casserole bits to get his beakers."

Comment:

You do not need a huge helping of psychobabble to enter, engage, and employ the forgiveness tools. To begin, you may have to empty yourself of leftovers from previous efforts to forgive. But you will not likely choke on anything, even if you have to swallow your pride or eat a little crow.

CHAPTER NINE

An Interlude

Making Contact: Maturity does make its demands. They need not be terribly imposing or overwhelming.

Story: I Resign (author unknown)

I AM HEREBY officially tendering my resignation as an adult. I have decided I would like to accept the responsibilities of an 8-year-old again. I want to go to McDonald's and think that it's a four-star restaurant. I want to sail sticks across a fresh mud puddle and make ripples with rocks. I want to think M&Ms are better than money because you can eat them. I want to lie under a big oak tree and run a lemonade stand with my friends on a hot summer day. I want to return to a time when life was simple, when all you knew were colors, multiplication tables, and nursery rhymes. But that didn't bother you because you didn't know what you didn't know and you didn't care. All you knew was to be happy because you were blissfully unaware of all the things that should make you worried or upset. I want to think the world is fair. That everyone is honest and good. I want to believe that anything is possible. I want to be oblivious to the complexities of life and be overly excited by the little things again. I want to live simply again. I don't want my day to consist of computer crashes, mountains of paperwork, depressing news, how to survive more days than there is money in the bank, doctor bills, gossip, illness, and loss of loved ones. I want to believe in the power of smiles, hugs, a kind word, truth, justice, peace, dreams, the imagination, mankind, and making angels in the snow.

So—here's my checkbook and my car keys, my credit card bills, and my 401K statements. I am officially resigning from adulthood. And if you want to discuss this further, you'll have to catch me first, because, "Tag you're it."

Pass it on…make someone else a kid again.

Comment:

We can become a new creation without becoming a child again if we reinvent the way we think about freedom and responsibility. As children, our freedom was restricted and we were taught to be responsible. At that time we probably felt more like an adult feels even though we differed in time and place. In the reverse way, adults are free to make choices that feel like childhood again. Doing so is more about our attitudes than what we decide to do. Our "I wants" as adults may differ in kind but need not differ in quality. Our beliefs need not confine us so there is no room for leisure, spontaneity, blissfulness, and simple pleasure. We can decide what to do with our day and how to live our years. We can make the boundaries that separate us from childhood firm or weak, wide or narrow, fixed or open. We are the architects of our lives and we can design the structure, prepare the blueprint, select the materials, and build until our hearts are content—at least as content as a child's.

You purchased this self-help book because you knew life could be better. You decided to help yourself live a better and more fulfilling life. You were willing to take responsibility for making it so.

Throughout this book you have been traveling the gateways to forgiveness. The steps may have been pondersome and laborious, but there have been small increments of progress. The distance traversed has closed the gap between you and another; you may now be within arms' length of the differences that separate you. Though not reaching to embrace one another, you stand face-to-face with a new reality that has been created by a desire to make love serve the interests of faith.

Discovering what has made a difference and what stands in the way of a more satisfying outcome is the primary aim of this interlude. We make the argument that the interplay of these gateways serve as fundamental and unifying elements in this process of forgiveness. They are both the means and the ends of forgiving. We will conclude this section of the book and then demonstrate how the outstretched arms of forgiveness can become the embracing joy of reconciliation (Chapter 9) and the basis for becoming a new creation (Chapter 10).

This book was also written to engage you, the reader, in a process presented as a series of gateways taking you down a road to recover part of yourself. Before we move on to the remaining two chapters, we want to revisit the process and review the criteria you can use to gauge your progress from one gateway to the next. We will emphasize the claims and counterclaims that constitute the struggle to forgive.

Baggage Claims

At the beginning, we invited you to accompany us on a journey to forgiveness. You packed your bags with unforgiving thoughts and un-forgiven emotions. The trip began by recognizing the strength it takes to travel with so much luggage. You packed behaviors that led you to seek retribution and to defend yourself against further hurt. You packed the weight of potent emotions such as anger and resentment toward the other person.

Neutralizing your behavioral disposition and negative feelings did take time, but as you read each chapter, time became your ally. You became actively involved in releasing yourself from the incapacitating grip of negative emotions so you could gradually develop positive behaviors toward your injurer. You began to unpack your bags and discard some items. While the trip became a little more manageable, you decided better safe than sorry and still took more than you needed.

Some gateways made greater claims on your time and energy and gave you more to see and do. You may have found yourself spending more time and emotional energy in Gateway One than Gateways Two or Three. Recall that Gateway One asked you to take an inventory of your reactions to the injury. One of these reactions was the use of psychological defense mechanisms, which are used to shield, protect, and distance us from pain. These mechanisms are insidious and, as such, require a high degree of openness and courage to overcome. Similarly, reacting to injury with anger is natural, but it is unnatural and unrealistic to begin the process of forgiveness without re-living memories of the event(s). The memories re-ignite the anger. Anger, though an emotion you are striving to release, does need to be legitimately expressed in order for it to subside.

You learned the inevitability of additional pain as you traversed the various pathways in your healing journey of forgiveness. As you gradually reclaimed yourself—your time, your energy, your person—you began to enjoy the journey free of the encumbrances of unforgiving attitudes, feelings, and actions.

Claims of Gateway One

In Gateway One, you became aware of your reactions to what the other person did to you—such as denial, anger, and resentment. We insisted that you must first claim the emotional reactions to your injury and then begin to work through them. You had to be honest and open with yourself about your feelings even though they were painful and heart-rending. We asked you to identify and examine some tools of deception. These were the defense mechanisms you might have been using to dull or avoid the pain. Abandoning the security and protection of this defense system may have been frightening. But having opened your luggage and surveyed the contents, you were ready to unpack the individual items. You began to wonder why in the world you packed so much and took along what was clearly unnecessary. This baggage check became a turning point in your preparation for the remainder of the journey.

Claims of Gateway Two

In Gateway Two, we asked you to deepen your awareness of your experience of pain by answering several questions: What happened? How did it happen? When did it happen? How often did it happen? Who did it? How did you feel at the time? How have you been feeling since it happened? And how are you feeling now? We impressed upon you that the more fully and honestly you answered these questions, the more determined you would be to resolve the source of your pain. We urged you to clutch your anger like a knife and cut through the dense fog that enveloped you. Restoring visibility enabled you to see beyond the immediate situation. Looking down the road enabled you to enter Gateway Three to search for ways to get rid of your pain.

Claims of Gateway Three

As you began searching for an antidote for your feelings of pain, you traveled farther and longer down the gateway toward forgiveness. You came upon a two-way intersection. At this crossroad, you could choose between intrapersonal or interpersonal understandings. As you explored the intrapersonal path, you discovered that you could numb your feelings of pain through physical activity (walking or jogging), social activity (calling or visiting a friend), or a pleasurable activity (reading a book or watching a movie). You found that your pain momentarily subsided, but it did not go away.

Was there another more permanent solution? You became curious about what taking the interpersonal path would have done for you. Armed with the prospect of a better you, you returned to the intersection and took an alternative route. As you traveled along the interpersonal path, you came to another two-way intersection. This time the fork in the road pointed toward justice or mercy.

At each of these intersections in the chapter, you had to make a choice. We helped you make the choice by asking reflective questions to make you cognizant of the costs and benefits of the routes you could take. We also cautioned you about the destructive outcomes of some choices. Finally, we claimed if you were inclined to choose forgiveness, you needed to continue your journey down Gateway Four.

Claims of Gateway Four

Gateway Four made new claims on you as your decision to forgive depended on your forgiveness style, social and family conditioning, the intensity of your pain, the passage of time since the injury occurred, a change of heart, or understanding that none of your past strategies has been effective and you were willing to give forgiveness a try.

Gateway Four helped you decide whether forgiveness was a viable option for you by first identifying your style of forgiving. You then examined how your culture helped or deterred you from choosing forgiveness. We encouraged you to reflect on how the use of forgiveness was modeled in your family. Although social and familial influences can be powerful inducements to extend or withhold forgiveness, we asserted that the more recent your injury and the more intense your pain was, the harder it would be for you to forgive, and vice versa. As you reflected on these issues, you may have experienced a reasonable degree of enthusiasm toward using forgiveness and even made a tentative decision to use it to free yourself from pain.

Claims of Gateways Five & Six

You may have begun to experience a sigh of relief the moment you consciously decided to forgive the person who hurt you. To sustain the sense of relief, we advised that you engage in a process called reframing. You'll recall that to reframe you needed to separate the person who caused you the pain from the pain itself. You might have discovered that you overlooked certain aspects that would have helped you understand what motivated your injurer to do what he/she did. We cautioned that you reframe to gain more understanding about the person rather than to condone or excuse what the person did to you. Reframing was just one of the tools of forgiveness that we suggested you use to unload your burden of pain. In Gateway Six, we described more tools.

In this most-involved Gateway, we provided you with a set of tools to use to strengthen your commitment to forgiving your injurer. We described each tool, delineated steps to using it, and provided you with precautions to keep in mind while implementing it. We maintained that your correct use of these tools would lead you to experience an increase in positive thoughts, feelings, and behaviors toward the person who caused you to join us in this journey of forgiveness. By the same token, incomplete or improper use of the tools would not have resulted in positive affect, thoughts, and behaviors toward your injurer. You would need to re-evaluate and re-use some of the tools to reach the final destination of your journey—forgiveness. You will experience a liberating internal release whereby your negative emotions of anger, resentment, and rage will decrease giving way to the positive emotions and thoughts to emerge. You will look at your injurer with a new pair of eyes—with understanding and compassion. Moreover, you may now begin to entertain the possibility of reconciling with the person from whom you have been estranged.

Reconciliation

What lies beyond forgiveness is the possibility of your reconciling with the person who hurt you. The claim that we made to you is that when you experience genuine feelings of forgiveness, these feelings open the gates toward reconciliation. They cause you to step beyond yourself and reach out to the very person who caused you undue pain and suffering in a humanistic embrace. However, you may find reconciliation to be either undesirable or impossible to consummate. It may be undesirable when you still feel that the person who hurt you has not changed his or her hurtful ways, and reconciling may put you at risk of that person's injurious behavior. Reconciling is impossible if the other person is either dead or nowhere to be found. Under such conditions, you may choose to enjoy the fruits of forgiveness and begin your renewed life of vitality, health, upbeat mood, and positive outlook on life.

Means and Ends to Forgiveness

Thus far in this book, we claimed that the process of forgiveness is for all healthy people who go through life seeking wholeness, oneness, and inclusiveness through more satisfying and fulfilling relationships. We intuitively understand that fulfillment is a quest, rather than a goal, for something beyond ourselves. We yearn for something beyond our grasp. You accepted the invitation because good health is at or near the top of your agenda for living.

It takes faith to begin the process, hope to sustain it, and love to crown it. As forgiveness springs in your heart, happy thoughts engulf your mind, and your arms stretch in loving embrace toward the other, please share the secret of forgiveness with others. Tell and assure them that human forgiveness, though slow and painful, is definitely possible.

Footnote:

Little Mikey was doing very badly in math. His parents had tried everything—tutors, flash cards, "Hooked on Math," everything they could think of. Finally, in a last ditch effort, they enrolled Mikey in the local Catholic school.

After the first day, Mikey came home with a very serious look on his face. He didn't kiss his mother hello. Instead, he went straight to his room and started studying. Books and paper were spread out all over the room and Mikey was hard at work. His mother was amazed.

She called him down to dinner and, to her shock, the minute he was done with dinner, he marched back to his room without a word and hit the books as hard as before. This went on day after day while the mother tried to understand what made all the difference.

Finally, Mikey brought home his report card. He quietly laid it on the table, went up to his room, and hit the books. With great trepidation his mom looked at the report card and, to her surprise, saw that Mikey had gotten an A in Math!

She could no longer hold her curiosity. She went to his room and asked, "Son, what was it? Was it the nuns?" Mikey looked at her and shook his head.

"Well then," she replied, "was it the books, the discipline, the structure, the uniforms, WHAT was it??"

Little Mikey looked at her and said, "Well, on the first day of school, when I saw that guy nailed to the plus sign, I knew they weren't fooling around."

Comment:

Sometimes nailing down just the right approach may be all it takes to turn a person around.

CHAPTER TEN

From Forgiveness to Reconciliation

*"Forgiveness does not change the past,
but it does enlarge the future."*

PAUL BOESE

Making Contact: Essence is in the struggle.

Story: Butterfly

A MAN FOUND a butterfly cocoon attached to a stick and took it home to watch it. One day a small opening appeared in the cocoon. The man sat and watched the butterfly for several hours as it struggled to force its body through that little hole.

Then the butterfly seemed to stop making any progress. It appeared as if it had gotten as far as it could and could go no further.

The man decided to help the butterfly. He used a pair of scissors to snip off the remaining bit of the cocoon.

The butterfly then emerged easily. But it had a swollen body and small, shriveled wings.

The man continued to watch the butterfly because he expected that, at any moment, the wings would enlarge and expand to support the body, which would contract in time.

Neither happened! In fact, the butterfly spent the rest of its life crawling around with a swollen body and shriveled wings. It never was able to fly.

What the man, in his kindness and haste, did not understand was that the restricting cocoon and the struggle required for the butterfly to get through the tiny opening were God's way of forcing fluid from the body of the butterfly into its wings so that it would be ready for flight once it achieved its freedom from the cocoon.

Sometimes struggles are exactly what we need in our lives. If God allowed us to go through our lives without any obstacles, it would cripple us.

We would not be as strong as what we could have been. We could never fly!

Comment:

Let us acknowledge at the outset that reconciliation is generally not all that easy. Knowing something about ourselves as human beings does help us understand why reconciliation can be difficult and what can be done to make it less so.

Reconciliation is seldom easy whether we initiate it or agree to it. It will generally be a struggle. We may work at easing the pain by trying to help the other person avoid the struggle. We may want to accept the full responsibility for the chasm that divides us if we can't stand to see the other person struggle with the problem. We underestimate their strength and ability to get things out into the open and deal with the aftermath of the struggle.

We may try to apply the techniques we have learned to snip away the last vestiges of unforgiveness. Once freed of these encumbrances before reconciliation, we believe the other person will be able to revive life in another form and another way. We regrettably learn that struggle is part of the process. Giving life and withholding life are integral parts of the same process. Where reconciliation works best, both parties are doing the work they have uniquely been given to do.

What is Reconciliation?

The word "reconcile" is derived from two Latin words (re-conciliare) that together mean "to reunite." One of the meanings Webster's Dictionary gives for "reconcile" is "to cause to be friendly again." Variations of these two meanings are given for the noun "reconciliation" including: (1) coming together with the offender in a manner that reflects the characteristics of the healing process that the offended has gone through (Hargrave, 1994); (2) reconnecting with someone who injured or offended us; and (3) the process of restoring a fractured relationship.

Comparing Reconciliation to Forgiveness

Reconciliation is described in the literature as a process that is personal, psychological, spiritual, and difficult. It may take a long time to achieve, and the outcomes are sometimes unpredictable. In the reconciliation process, the forgiver makes the choice to reach out to the other and endeavors to tear down the many walls that have been built between the forgiver and forgiven. When a person truly forgives another person, at least three outcomes occur (Smedes,1984): rediscovering the humanity of the offender; surrendering our right to seek revenge; and the third, which relates directly to reconciliation, revising our feelings toward the individual and being open to a new relationship built on mutual respect with the person who wronged us. Reconciliation then goes beyond forgiveness which can occur without even speaking to the offending party. Seeking reconciliation, however, involves an effort to mend and/or re-establish a relationship that has gone sour. While forgiveness is the first step toward undoing what has been done, reconciliation can be a second step to getting something done because it matters to both parties.

Forgiveness is essentially an *intrapersonal* transaction of looking, searching, and healing within oneself. Reconciliation is an *interpersonal* encounter. It requires reaching with forgiveness beyond forgiveness to bring about something both parties can live with and live by. Reconciliation can only occur when collaboration and conciliation are placed in the service of getting back together to find new ways to live together. Forgiveness paves the way for reconciliation. The destination for forgiveness is "I am okay and wish you well" whereas the destination for reconciliation is "we're okay and wish each other well." Reconciliation completes the healing journey for both parties.

Prerequisites to Reconciliation

Before a person decides to go the distance in the process of reconciliation, it is best to pack one's bags and be clothed in the following prerequisites:

1. Be thoroughly aware of what caused the relationship to break down.
2. Examine whether it is possible to reconcile with the other.
3. Examine whether it is safe (physically, psychologically, and morally) to reconcile with the other.
4. Determine one's motives for reconciliation.
5. Ascertain one's readiness for the journey of reconciliation.
6. Pursue the reconciliation route willingly.

Each of these prerequisites is discussed next in more detail.

What Caused the Rift in the Relationship?

You must be honest in your answer to this question. You need to remember exactly what the other person did to you, when, and where. Describing the situation, relying entirely on the facts, you merely acknowledge what happened. There is no attempt to evaluate or assign responsibility for what happened.

Is it Possible to Reconcile with the Other?

Here evaluation enters the process. You must decide whether there is a reasonable chance this person would want to: (1) repair what has been broken; (2) bring the glue and the shattered pieces; and (3) offer another pair of hands to hold these pieces in place. Sometimes it is not possible to reconcile with the person who hurt you either because he/she is deceased or cannot be found. In this case, writing one's thoughts of reconciliation in a letter format on sharing one's feelings with a separate person who knew both of you might be your only recourse. You can only indirectly reconnect with the person by refurbishing the bonds that once sealed your relationship.

Is it Safe to Reconcile with the Other?

This is a very critical question to think deeply and thoroughly about. If the injurer remains defiant and vindictive, it may not be wise to reconnect with him or her. For example, if your ex-spouse or friend continues to blame you, hold a grudge, or seek revenge, it won't be safe to approach this person. You will likely be opening yourself to abusive remarks, possibly physical injury. Moreover, you might find yourself facing a crisis of forgiveness all over again. That is, you will have go through the steps of forgiveness to deal with a renewed sense of unfairness and the will to release the injurer once again. Going through forgiveness once is arduous enough. Having to go through it again for a repeated offense by the same perpetrator makes forgiving ever more difficult. The second time you may even feel it was a mistake to be forgiving of the original offense.

Why Do You Want to Reconcile?

Are you reconciling for the right reasons? What are your reasons? Are they prompted by a genuine interest and desire to renew the relationship in the interest of preserving the self-respect and dignity of both parties? In committing to reconciliation, you need to be somewhat cautious about justifying your reasons if you have an unconscious negative tendency for superiority and requiring accountability to what happened.

Are You Ready to Reconcile?

Prepare yourself to be fully ready to embark on the process of reconciliation. This means that you have successfully and genuinely forgiven the person who hurt you and that you feel it is both possible and safe to reconcile with the injurer. Like forgiving, reconciling takes courage and humility because you do not know what the other party will bring to the table and how you will deal with the uncertainty. There will be some testing of sincerity and honesty and some sparring for control. This is unfamiliar ground for both parties. Both of you are likely to walk tentatively at first.

Are You Willing to Reconcile?

Equally important, you must also be willing to take up the cause of reconciliation by making a decision free of threat and intimidation. Your decision should include an undercurrent of goodwill. You should be inwardly convinced and optimistic that the reconciliation experience will be essential to your own and the other person's growth and well-being. The following questionnaire might help you decide whether you are ready to reconcile:

Laura Davis's 2002 *"Are You Ready for Reconciliation Questionnaire"*

Circle the number beneath each question that indicates your current feelings. If your response is a strong "no" or "yes," circle numbers at either end of the scale. If your answers are more mixed, choose a number in the middle that most accurately reflects where you are today.

1. Has a relationship with someone you once cared about ended because of anger, betrayal, or miscommunication?
   1   2   3   4   5   6   7   8   9   10
   no   yes

2. Do you miss the other person and wish he or she could still be in your life?
   1   2   3   4   5   6   7   8   9   10
   no   yes

3. Have you worked through your own feelings enough to approach this person in a new way?
   1   2   3   4   5   6   7   8   9   10
   no   yes

4. Are you ready to take responsibility for your role in what happened?
   1   2   3   4   5   6   7   8   9   10
   no   yes

5. Have you developed a sense of compassion for the other person?
   1   2   3   4   5   6   7   8   9   10
   no   yes

6. Have you moved beyond fantasies of revenge and retaliation?
   1   2   3   4   5   6   7   8   9   10
   no   yes

7. Could you move forward even if you receive no apology or acknowledgment that you were wronged?
   1   2   3   4   5   6   7   8   9   10
   no   yes

8. Are you being realistic about the other person? Have you stopped pinning your hope on a fantasy?
   1   2   3   4   5   6   7   8   9   10
   no   yes

9. If a limited relationship is all that is possible, would that be acceptable to you?
   1   2   3   4   5   6   7   8   9   10
   no   yes

10. Can you be in this relationship and still feel good about yourself?

    1   2   3   4   5   6   7   8   9   10

    no   yes

11. Given the risks involved in reaching out, are you willing to face the worst possible scenario?

    1   2   3   4   5   6   7   8   9   10

    no   yes

12. Do you have what it takes to rebuild this relationship?

    1   2   3   4   5   6   7   8   9   10

    no   yes

If the majority of your answers cluster around the "yes" end of the scale, it's a good indicator that you are ready to pursue reconciliation. Answers that cluster around the "no" end of the scale point out issues you may need to resolve before you will be ready to reach out to the other person.

In summary, as you consider the implications of reconciliation, the above factors are useful guidelines. They increase the likelihood that your efforts will be fruitful and satisfying. Bear in mind as you begin the process you need to be patient and persistent. This process will take time because touching the hurts and healing the wounds does not happen overnight. Both of you will have to walk from darkness into light. You will need to see and act anew. It takes time to restore trust and confidence in the other. The next section builds further on these primary elements using a four-fold approach that engages you with the person who injured you.

Types or Levels of Reconciliation

After considering the prerequisites to reconciliation, you'll want to know about the distinct levels or types of reconciliation that can transpire. In his 2004 book, *From Conflict Resolution to Reconciliation*, Marc Ross indicated that "reconciliation is best understood as a continuum, meaning that there can be degrees of reconciliation..." (p.44). Ross also differentiated between strong and weak types of reconciliation. Strong reconciliation entails a total transformation in the relationship between the victim and victimizer. Weak reconciliation, by comparison, produces only enough change in the relationship so as to allow for normal and constructive interactions.

According to Laura Davis, the reconciliation continuum consists of four specific levels. The first type is deep and transformative reconciliation. This is the ideal, but most difficult type to achieve. This reconciliation is achieved when you and the person who hurt you establish or re-establish intimacy, resolve your past transgressions, and begin to experience closeness, satisfaction, and renewed growth in your relationship. You and the other person experience a rebirth in the relationship that is now characterized by mutual respect, trust, and deep understanding.

In the second type, at least one party involved spurns the reconciliation attempt by a change in perspective and expectations. This is the most common type of reconciliation, which occurs after the person who was hurt has forgiven the person who hurt him/her. Even though the injured party is rejected, that person now looks at the other person with a new lens, a new pair of eyes, as Smedes aptly described it in his Forgive & Forget book. As the person's perspective of the injurer changes, so do the possibilities for a renewed relationship. Now, you accept the other person's limitations and proclivities. You no longer insist on seeing significant changes in the other person before you are willing to reconcile with him/her.

Agree-to-Disagree reconciliation is the third type of reconciliation. At this level of reconciliation, many aspects of the relationship between you and the other person remain unresolved. Both of you continue to have persistent and ambivalent feelings toward each other. The distinguishing feature and hallmark of this reconciliation level is that you both agree to disagree. You enjoy cordial relations based on ground rules that you both establish in order to have a peaceful co-existence. An example of this is a divorced couple who share custody of their children and reconcile in this way for the sake of their children.

The fourth and final type of reconciliation described is the "no viable relationship is possible" reconciliation. You figure out that the other person is either uninterested in or not ready for a renewed relationship at this time. Or it may not be possible or safe to reconcile with him or her. Your only option is to find resolution within yourself—to be content in your heart and mind with the positive attitude and emotions that you have toward the other person.

Keep in mind that the reconciliation process is very dynamic, fluid, and unpredictable. The outcomes of reconciliation run the gamut. At the beginning, you may have a limited, social relationship with the other person, and later the relationship may become deeper and more intimate. There are also surprises and setbacks that accompany this tenuous and sensitive process. A minor offense from either you or the other person may threaten to tear apart the young, healing relationship, leaving you estranged from each other once again.

Steps Toward Reconciliation

Here we'll describe four fundamental steps to follow before reaching out toward the other person. These steps were described by Simon & Simon in their 1990 book, *Forgiveness: How to Make Peace with Your Past and Get On With Your Life.*

Step One: Define the Relationship

Define carefully the kind of relationship you wish to have with your injurer. This important step is a decision-making process where you draw the parameters of the kind of relationship that suits you. You begin by searching for answers to the question: "What do I really want the restored relationship to be like?" It is here where you need to set reasonable, realistic, and attainable expectations. For example, if your ex-spouse had abused you physically or emotionally before, what is it that you would expect to be different in the relationship? To set your expectations, try making a list of the "good reasons" and "bad reasons" for wanting to patch up and renew your relationship with the abusive person. Then define the type of relationship you wish to have by asking yourself the following questions:

1. What is the nature of my relationship with the other person now? Do we occasionally see each other? Do we talk on the phone, over the internet, or indirectly hear about each other through friends or relatives? How does the other person perceive me? Does he/she avoid me? Does he/she make attempts to talk with me? Describe all the characteristics and conditions that define the relationship as it exists now.
2. What type of relationship do I ideally aspire to have with the other person? That is, what types of changes would I like to see in the other person that would make it easier and more attractive for me to reconnect with that person? What changes in me might be necessary to elicit and support the behavior I want from the other person?
3. After you identify the current condition of the relationship, state the ideal one that you wish for, then describe in as much detail as you can the type of relationship that you can realistically have. Here, you must examine yourself as a person who has gone through the forgiveness process. Ask yourself: How have I emerged from this process, particularly in the way I view myself and the other person? What changes have taken place in the other person, if any? Has the other person gone through changes that increase the likelihood of reconciliation? We cannot realistically expect the other person to be exactly what we wish him/her to be. It is crucial to think realistically about the qualities or conditions that would be most satisfying for you and this person as you try to begin anew.

Step Two: Ways to Reach Your Goal

In the second step, after you have set your goal as a realistic relationship and one you can live with, think about how you want to go about achieving that objective. The issues that you must consider include methods that you will employ to contact the other person. How will you approach him or her? Is it going to be a face-to-face meeting? Where will you meet? Should you consider a public place? Will you meet alone without a mediator or other people around? If you decide to meet the other person, what sorts of things do you want to say and avoid saying? What will you make of the past, present, and the future? How will you say them? As you brainstorm about what you want to say to the other person, it is very important for you to anticipate how the person will respond and react to what you say and do. More specifically, you must think about how you will respond if the other person does not behave or react in the manner that you anticipated or desired?

Your aim in this step, then, is to think of the ways by which you can best achieve your goal and to carefully consider the consequences of each aspect of your goal-achieving strategy. You must remember that approaching the other person whom you have not talked to or dealt with for a period of time is anxiety provoking so you need to think of the best means that suit you. Visualizing the interaction before actually meeting the other person can be helpful. You may want to think about and rehearse the points you want to express to the other person. Sometimes it might be easier, safer, and much more comfortable to establish contact through a letter or e-mail before having a face-to-face meeting.

Since you cannot be sure how the conversation will unfold, you may be reticent to even begin thinking about getting together. The process can also be distressing so you may be reluctant to make the initial contact. And the process may be lengthy, so proceed patiently and without high expectations. Make decisions slowly that may include taking well-intentioned and purposeful risks. It will help to anticipate disappointments. Finally, make sure that you have a backup network or support system to help you prepare and reflect upon your plans.

Step Three: Solicit Emotional Support.

As you decide on a plan of action for reconciling with another, it is advisable to have the emotional support from friends and loved ones who can make this process less unnerving and possibly more fruitful. Emotional support will be most efficacious when the meeting with the other person falls short of your expectations, or worse yet, when the outcome of your initial session is disappointing. If the interaction is negative, you may experience a resurgence of the earlier conflict and emotional upset. Trusted friends, relatives, or a professional counselor could help you bridge the differences between what you had hoped for and the actual result.

Regardless of your best laid plans, you may neglect the obvious and regret the unforeseen. Thus, it would be wise to discuss your plans and goals for reconciliation with a trusted friend before, during, and after contacting the person with whom you want to reconcile. Provision for ongoing support does help establish a secure and stable base from which to work. Providing the needed support is a people-driven activity. Be certain this notion activates your thinking and influences your decisions as you solicit emotional support. When you do think about whom to rely on for emotional support, you may want to consider the following:

- Whom can I rely on for unconditional and non-judgmental support during this process?
- Whom can I turn to for guidance and wise counsel? Is there someone who knows both me and the other and would honestly help me look objectively at this situation?
- Whom do I want support from before, during, and after contacting the other person?

Step Four: Anticipate the Unknown

Since you do not know how things will turn out as you plan to approach the other person, it is all the more important that you reduce as much uncertainty in the situation as possible. You might even weigh in on the optimistic side of your plans. What is there about this person and the intervening period that might contribute to the process of this effort at reconciliation? Is it possible that the person with whom you would like to recover a relationship will meet or surpass your expectations? Success does not depend entirely on your preparation. Doing your part is only one side of the equation. Do not underestimate the goodwill and cordiality that once defined your relationship. This person may just be waiting for you to take the first step. He/she may feel awkward about initiating the process. Or it may be a waiting game. Someone has to make the first move only to learn that the two of you are not that far apart. It is even possible the other person will offer you an apology for what he or she did to you. In other words, the person will acknowledge his/her role in the relationship rift and express a will to do what he/she can to mend it.

The opposite can also happen. The person who hurt you may say it was a mistake or is denying what "really" happened. The person may get upset, mad, or angry when feeling accused or blamed. This is part of the calculated risk you take as you seek reconciliation. All you can control are your own words and actions. You can take comfort knowing there is a chance that comparing "notes" with the other person can help you reconcile the clash, reframe the conflict, and resolve your differences.

If the initial efforts at reconciliation fail, you can review view your side of the problem and assess your strategy for resolution. You may need to think of alternative means to accomplish the goal(s) you set. Consider the following scenario.

> When Mary decided that she would rather meet in person with her friend, Sally, who betrayed her trust, she thought that meeting in a restaurant for coffee would be a good place for their first reconciliation meeting. That proved to be a disaster. As Mary began to execute her plan of telling Sally that she wanted to meet with her to tell her that she forgave her for divulging a confidence several years ago, Sally reacted angrily and started shouting at Mary. Sally yelled, "How dare you accuse me of something I did not do? How dare you bring me to a public place and discuss a matter like this in public! You must want to embarrass me in front of other people!"
>
> Mary did not anticipate Sally's reaction, and she spent most of the time apologizing to Sally for doing it this way. Mary reiterated that her intention behind the meeting was a desire to restore the trust and relationship she once had with Sally. Sally was not the least bit interested in dealing with Mary's issue at this time. Mary was disappointed and did not want to try talking to Sally again. As a matter of fact, Mary began to experience some of the negative emotions she went through to forgive her best friend Sally.

Sally's reactions are not uncommon for a first interaction. Sally was not ready for reconciliation as she had not yet acknowledged her role in the fractured relationship. When might Sally be ready? Maybe never. Should Mary give up? The answer is "No." Mary may not want to talk to Sally any time soon, but she should consider a different plan of action and give the process time. Mary should persist until she exhausts all the possibilities. She will at least be happy that she has given the process her best. Mary cannot force Sally to reconcile with her. Just as it is a choice for Mary to seek reconciliation, it is also a choice for Sally to accept or reject the invitation to go through the reconciliation journey.

Obstacles to Reconciliation

As we saw in Mary's example, the major obstacle to reconciliation is the failure of the offending party to take responsibility for the harm he/she caused the victim. The injurer usually avoids accepting blame for the offense by using the following strategies: (1) deny responsibility; (2) deny that harm was actually done; (3) deny the worth of the victim; (4) attack the accuser; and (5) claim that he/she was acting in the service of a higher cause. Let's look at each of these strategies.

Denial of Responsibility

Denying responsibility for an offense committed against us inspires little, if any, motivation in us to reconcile with the other. The other person's denial deals a very strong blow to us and shatters our sense of moral expectations and sensibilities. Thus, such denial of responsibility and failure to acknowledge the wrong done has the potential to widen the rift in the relationship.

If the other person does not own up to his/her role in our injury, the process of reconciliation cannot continue. The injurer may be unwilling to take the blame because he/she fears losing a sense of power in the relationship, or losing face. In other words, the injurer may be withholding acknowledgment of responsibility to protect his/her own sense of self, dignity, and pride. The person may also feel that it is not safe for him/her to move away from the stated position for fear of being perceived as weak. We must then choose to wait until the other person is ready to acknowledge what he/she has done.

When the other person feels threatened and fears losing face, efforts to save face overrule the substantive and central issue in the interpersonal conflict. In this case, authors Folger, Poole & Stutman in their 2001 book Working Through Conflict recommend the use of "preventive practices" to prevent or minimize threats to the other person's face. In the context of reconciliation, if it becomes apparent that the other person is afraid of losing face by taking the blame, we must do our best to support his/her personal image with magnanimity and humility.

Denial that Harm Was Done

Another form of justification the injurer may use is to admit responsibility for the hurt he/she incurred on you, but deny that harm was actually done. You will naturally perceive this behavior as insensitive, irresponsible, and arrogant. You may wonder who gives this person the right to minimize the extent of injury to you. In a way, denying that harm was done adds insult to your injury. You would expect the other person to give you a sincere apology that may begin to cleanse your hurt and heal your relationship with him/her. But when you get a denial or dishonest admission of responsibility without heart-felt remorse, reconciliation is not on the negotiation table.

By denying that harm was done, the other person communicates to us his/her lack of respect, care, and empathy for us, thereby again significantly reducing our desire for reconciliation. We must remember though that it takes time, courage, and wisdom for a person to say "I'm sorry" for the hurt he/she caused. The person must work through his/her fears and resistance before acknowledging the hurt incurred. Hopefully, when the proud person admits that he/she hurt you and apologizes for it, the apology will be accompanied by a change in behavior. Sincere words of apology followed by sincere actions make reconciliation more possible. Bhikkhu in his 2004 article, Reconciliation: Right & Wrong described the act of admitting one's mistakes to others as a prerequisite to achieving purity in thought, word, and deed. By recognizing their mistakes and altering their behavior, the wrong doers illuminate "the world like the moon when freed from a cloud," (p. 4).

Denial of Victim's Worth

This third obstacle to reconciliation attacks the dignity and self-worth of the victim. This obstacle is by no means a conciliatory act and reeks of an absence of goodwill toward the victim. Furthermore, denying the victim's worth does not signal good intentions, express a wish to build a peaceful relationship, or exhibit sensitivity to the other person's feelings, thoughts, needs, and aspirations.

The victim may justifiably feel de-legitimized, still demonized by the injurer and thwarted from pursuing reconciliation. If the offender shows feelings of superiority in response to the victim's gesture of reconciliation, it is wise not to engage the offender and pursue reconciliation. In this case, the injurer is displaying the signs and symptoms of ill-will and downright animosity.

Reconciliation can only take place when the other participant is receptive and willing to do his/her part in the reconciliation process. Dealing with the victim in a way that diminishes his/her dignity is all but a sign of the offender's refusal to accept the gift of reconciliation. Resumption of the relationship is not possible under these circumstances. This may not be the time to say "hello" but rather the time to say "good bye" for now. The victim may feel that reconciliation is still a possibility sometime down the line.

Attacking the Accuser

If the other person acts belligerent and nasty toward the victim's overtures of reconciliation, reconciliation is also unlikely in this circumstance. A victim has gotten over the hurt and pain of the initial injury does not want to be exposed to more hurt, agony, and heartache.

Whether the attack is physical or verbal, it is unsafe and unhealthy for the injured party to pursue reconciliation at this time. Resolution within yourself is all you can have at this time. If this interaction occurs between friends, spouses, parent-child, boss-employee, or any other setting, the wise thing to do is to avoid contact with the other person in order to safeguard yourself against any attack to your physical or psychological well-being.

However, if you are perceived as the accuser, it is perfectly clear that you have now become the person who should apologize and show remorse and guilt for something you have not done. This is an effort on the other person's part to portray him/herself as the victim, not the offender. Now you stand accused of being the offending party. This is an unfair and unjust twisting of reality which is best left alone.

Acting in Service of a Higher Cause

The fifth and final obstacle takes a more sinister form. The other person feels justified in his/her past treatment toward you because he/she was acting in the service of a higher cause, whatever that may be. This is a self-deceptive mechanism that the other person uses to justify his/her hurtful actions. Abusing, humiliating, disappointing, betraying, brutalizing, or any unfair act that brings harm to the other person are not warranted and unjustifiable. What higher cause is served by inhumane and brutal acts?

An individual who uses the service to a higher cause argument admits what he/she did but believes that he/she is ordained to carry out that mission.

These five obstacles are all indicators that reconciliation is not possible, safe, or healthy to pursue. As long as the other person remains stuck in the denial mental set, you are better off to celebrate the resolution that forgiveness has produced within yourself. Not every broken relationship can be reestablished and healed.

Consequences of Reconciliation

Like forgiveness, reconciliation has many advantages. Reconciliation closes the curtain to the painful past and leads the involved parties from estrangement to peace. In the climate of peace, the injured and injurer expose and talk about what happened and both let go of the past events in favor of a restored and healed relationship. The reconciling participants also recognize the need to redress the wrong as they move toward a renewed relationship.

Forgiveness reopens the future for the victim and his/her offender. This, in the words of David Augsburger in an article published in 2000, "is the consequence of transforming the memory from a wound that will not heal to a wound that has healing power within the soul," (p.1). In reconciling, participants begin to build a relationship based on renewed trust and mutual respect. Laura Davis reported that many people who successfully reconciled told her how rewarding reconciliation is. More specifically, they said they now have " a deeper sense of compassion, restored faith in human decency, and renewed bonds of love" (p. 311). Other rewards of reconciliation include learning more effective, respectful, and empowering communication skills such as listening non-judgmentally and compassionately, and working more resourcefully and fairly through differences.

Freedom from estrangement is probably one of the most commonly reported advantages of reconciliation, especially for participants in the deep and transformative type of reconciliation. They no longer have to be obsessed with the feeling of discomfort and the remorse and sorrow it produces. Also, as the reconcilers enjoy their newly restored relationship, they happily bid farewell to the devastating and excruciating sense of isolation and loneliness that accompanies estrangement. Furthermore, as the relationship resumes, the persons involved learn not to take their fragile relationship for granted, so they jealously guard it and nurture it with care.

Other consequences of reconciliation include promoting harmony in the community and allowing the reconciling parties to participate more effectively in the community. If the reconcilers are family members, the rift that separated them is bridged and there's no longer a need to create alliances and worry about divided loyalties. The family and the rest of the community crown the reconciliation process by celebrating the renewed acceptance and mutual affirmation. The celebration will be a way to publicly release the pain that tore not only the two individuals involved but the entire community.

Summary and Conclusion

As you went through the forgiveness steps, you worked through the baggage of the past and hopefully emerged rich with goodwill toward the person who hurt you. Just as you willingly and willfully underwent the forgiveness journey, you may have chosen to pursue the goal of reconciliation. This chapter offered you guidelines to consider and follow as you seek to share the goodwill of forgiveness in the act of reconciliation. By doing so, you can close the door to the painful past and open the gates wide with the hope for a better future. You can open your arms in a heartfelt embrace to the person from whom you became physically and psychologically estranged, alienated, and separated.

In the reconciliation process, the following four powerful forces intersect and fuse: truth manifested by acknowledgement, transparency, revelation, and clarity; mercy displayed through acceptance, forgiveness, support, compassion, and healing; justice exhibited through equality, right relationship, rectification, and restitution; and peace shown in harmony, unity, well-being, security, and respect.

Footnote:

A man is driving down the road and his car breaks down near a monastery. He goes to the monastery, knocks on the door, and says, "My car broke down. Do you think I could stay the night?"

The monks graciously accept him, feed him dinner, even fix his car. As the man tries to fall asleep, he hears a strange sound. The next morning, he asks the monks what the sound was, but they say, "We can't tell you. You're not a monk."

The man is disappointed but thanks them anyway and goes on his merry way.

Some years later, the same man's car breaks down in front of the same monastery. The monks accept him, feed him, and even fix his car. That night, he hears the same strange noise that he had heard years earlier. The next morning, he asks what it is, but the monks reply, "We can't tell you. You're not a monk."

The man says, "All right, all right. I'm dying to know. If the only way I can find out what that sound was is to become a monk, how do I become a monk?"

The monks reply, "You must travel the earth and tell us how many blades of grass there are and the exact number of sand pebbles. When you find these numbers, you will become a monk."

The man sets about his task. Forty-five years later, he returns and knocks on the door of the monastery. He says, "I have traveled the earth and have found what you have asked for. There are 145,236,284,232 blades of grass and 231,281,219,999, 129,382 sand pebbles on the earth."

The monks reply, "Congratulations. You are now a monk. We shall now show you the way to the sound."

The monks lead the man to a wooden door, where the head monk says, "The sound is right behind that door."

The man reaches for the knob, but the door is locked. He says, "Real funny. May I have the key?"

The monks give him the key, and he opens the door. Behind the wooden door is another door made of stone. The man demands the key to the stone door. The monks give him the key and he opens it, only to find a door made of ruby. He demands another key from the monks, who provide it. Behind that door is another door, this one made of sapphire. So it went until the man had gone through doors of emerald, silver, topaz, amethyst…

Finally, the monks say, "This is that last key to the last door."

The man is relieved to no end. He unlocks the door, turns the knob, and behind that door he is amazed to find the source of that strange sound. But I can't tell you what it is because you're not a monk.

Comment:

As strange as it might seem, when it comes to reconciliation, no one can tell you what it is like. You must find out for yourself. This might require an exhausting regimen only the most determined can undertake and persevere.

Forgiveness is only the beginning but it does supply some of the keys to reconciliation. You can begin to open some of the doors that have been locked over the years. You will know when you are about to gain entry into the fullness of reconciliation when you pass behind the doors of precious jewels. Eventually you will open the final door. You will see the source of all your curiosity and striving. No one can tell you what it is like. You have to find out for yourself.

CHAPTER ELEVEN

Beyond Forgiveness & Reconciliation: Becoming a New Creation

Making Contact: Virtues as instruments of vision and vitality.

Story:

A PROFESSOR STOOD before his philosophy class with some items in front of him. When the class began, wordlessly, he picked up a very large, empty mayonnaise jar and filled it with golf balls. He then asked the students if the jar was full. They agreed that it was.

So the professor picked up a box of pebbles and poured them into the jar. He shook the jar lightly. The pebbles rolled into the open areas between the golf balls. He then asked the students again if the jar was full. They agreed it was.

The professor next picked up a box of sand and poured it into the jar. Of course, the sand filled up everything else. He asked once more if the jar was full. The students responded with an unanimous "yes."

The professor then produced two cans of beer from under the table and poured the entire contents into the jar, effectively filling the empty space between the sand. The students laughed.

"Now," said the professor, as the laughter subsided, "I want you to recognize that this jar represents your life. The golf balls are the important things—your family, your children, your health, your friends, your favorite passions—things that if everything else was lost and only they remained, your life would still be full.

"The pebbles are the other things that matter like your job, your house, your car. The sand is everything else—the small stuff?"

"If you put the sand in the jar first," he continued, "there is no room for the pebbles or the golf balls. The same goes for life. If you spend all your time and energy on the small stuff, you will never have room for the things that are important to you. Pay attention to the things that are critical to your happiness. Play with your children. Take time to get medical checkups. Take your partner out to dinner. Play another 18.

"There will always be time to clean the house and fix the disposal. Take care of the golf balls first, the things that really matter. Set your priorities. The rest is just sand."

One of the students raised her hand and inquired what the beer represented.

The professor smiled. "I'm glad you asked. It just goes to show you that no matter how full your life may seem, there's always room for a couple of beers."

Comment:

Virtues are the big stuff of life. They invite us to choose wisely and prudently. They leave plenty of room for the small stuff, like grains of sand that easily pass through our fingers with an unknown destination. Virtues, on the other hand, do point us in a particular direction and provide us a compass for getting to a variety of destinations. Virtues are purposeful entities and can have a profound influence upon the way we see and regard the world. They are calibrated so we can measure and check for compliance. The gradations on the scale of virtue permit us to gradually define, cultivate, and become the virtue. We become what we have chosen and live what we want to be.

Virtues can also be regarded as a platform to stand upon as we seek a better world view. We can see more and farther when virtues are used as a launching pad for living. We can all stand tall, confident, and secure when virtues supply a rock solid foundation for our living. Occasional tremors will only mildly affect us. We bear up well when the winds blow in all directions, and we're not subjected to the furrows and ruts when the heavy rains come. We can drink to our success when we take a stand and live what it requires.

A Preamble

We are shaped or formed from the inside and influenced from the outside. Our convictions to our established values and virtues emanate from our loyalty to a community and coalesce as an ideal way of relating to one another. Our culture strongly influences these relationships by teaching us the behaviors to most appropriately express this internalized way of thinking and feeling. We grow in personal understanding as we try to reconcile these two sources of growth—convictions and culture. We learn to use our internal frame-of-reference (values, convictions) to weigh the importance and evaluate the consistency between our beliefs and our behaviors. Any discrepancy between these two may make us feel tense and uncomfortable. Like a detective in such a case, we set out to solve the "crime" and try to reduce the tension by finding the culprit. But, whatever evidence we find is not always completely accurate and convincing. Instead, we often "convict" the internal condition (values) because it cannot resist our accusations. But being accused and getting a "conviction" depends upon some good police work.

Values and virtues can twist the evidence to justify themselves as they rely upon reason for their existence. And it is reason that comes to their defense. Behaviors, on the other hand, are just that—behaviors or actions that merely serve the values and virtues. When values and virtues insist on having their way, behaviors capitulate. However, even behaviors can fight back when public mores enable a person to look the other way. In that case, we think ourselves into and out of a jam by using the power of public opinion to defend the practice. People cheat on their taxes and defend the practice by claiming everyone does it. Honesty is supposedly not compromised because society has provided an excuse. Virtues and values struggle for survival when we make decisions using costs and benefits analysis. Tangible benefits and intangible costs favor the former behaviors.

Through rehabilitation we seek to achieve a maturity where our inside values and virtues and outside behaviors work in harmony. But getting there may mean a constant struggle to be ourselves and behave ourselves. Even so, the struggle indicates that we are trying to reconcile an abstract (value) and a concrete reality (behavior). We are trying to make the message a rock-bed commitment to a virtue. Our virtues cannot be purchased or changed because they are not subject to the enticements of a world that claims the means justify the ends. Rather, the end for our rehabilitation is always an integrated, whole self, anchored in integrity. This chapter will look at how we can get there using a number of virtues that serve as standards to help us make our way into a virtuous life. They serve as sentinels always on guard at the entrance to our home. They serve as a compass that gives us direction when we set out each day and return each night. They serve as a beacon of light to help us discover and discern the meaning and purpose in life. Virtues are our life-line that keep us from drifting off into the dizzying array of choices that lap at the shoreline of our lives.

What then are the virtues that provide a stabilizing influence in our lives? What is the work virtues do and how do we know when they are serving their purpose? How do we deal with attacks on our virtues and recover from the setbacks we encounter when we stray from the ideals they work to preserve? While our virtues give us a means to question life, life also challenges our virtues as we try to live them. Ultimately we are defined by the virtues we prize and honor day-to-day over the course of a lifetime.

A Recapitulation

The pages of this book were devoted to a process whereby you became healthier and more virtuous. You have taken steps to restore and renew something that bears the signature of someone committed to growth in the virtuous ways of living. You worked toward forgiveness using an alliance of virtues bent upon making peace with yourself and another. You restored and renewed loving yourself and others beyond your pain. In doing so, you progressively moved out and away from something that held you in the grip of alienation so that you did not belong to yourself in a satisfying way. Something unfinished lurked in the background and cast a shadow over your life and hid the pain of bitterness, resentment, disillusionment, and despair. But your decision to step out of the shadow and become a son or daughter of the light showed you the truth of who you are and who you want to be. You no longer feel like an outsider, unfamiliar with what bothers and troubles you. You have crossed a chasm and taken up your life on the other side of alienation. Now, no longer separated from the best you have to offer, you can also receive the best of what others have to give.

Making your way from un-forgiveness to forgiveness is one route to the virtuous life. It is like an exodus journey because crossing over to the promised land includes the hardships of the desert. You know what it is like to be dry. You have reached down into the deep well of compassion and struggled to draw up the bucket. You learned that at times you had to deal with a leaky bucket or one with contents insufficient to quench your thirst. At other times you just fought to survive—there was little that you could do beyond caring for yourself. Yet the longer you persisted in your quest, the greater the likelihood you reached your promised land of forgiveness.

We all want to go to a place of wheat and honey, a place where we have all the ingredients to make the bread of life. When we reach that place, we know we are stronger, happier, and more content for having persisted. We want to remain in this place to live the fullness of our new life.

You knew early on you would be crossing the desert. The preparation began before you bought this book. Something drew you toward forgiveness and that became the purpose for your pilgrimage. A number of virtues became midwives. They came to assist the life-giving process and deliver on the promise of a new birth. The midwife helped you draw upon this new birth and make these virtues, as you made forgiveness, the centerpiece in your new life. Forgiving behaviors were chosen, learned, and demonstrated as applications of these virtues. You *behaved* yourself into a deeper commitment to and a more formidable expression of these virtues. The interplay between these two actions brought about a more considerate and consistent you.

In this chapter, we will name and examine these virtues. We will look specifically at the contributions they make to instigating, inspiring, and sustaining the forgiveness process. Virtues can be a wellspring of strength from which you draw. They can also inoculate you against variations of anger and fear as responses to physical trauma and psychological afflictions of the mind, heart, and soul.

You long ago planted the seeds of virtue in good ground. You have tried, provided, and monitored the conditions that would maximize the fruits of your labor. You probably have been more or less attentive to some seeds. Picture the person who was raised in a competitive and success driven family and is unable to maximize the fruits of patience. Life was urgent and immediacy was prized. He learned to be uneasy in situations where change was hampered by endless discussions, fruitless debates, and avoidable delays. This unbridled restlessness led to frustration, particularly when layers of bureaucracy dampened spirits and ultimately fostered indifference. He believes in a no nonsense approach to management and leaves little time to cultivate patience which requires listening to the heart. It would take a radical change in the rhythm of life for this man to acquire habits of thought and practice to take the frenzy out of living and rest long enough to be rooted in patience.

Picture the woman who has been raised in a close-knit family rooted in loyalty. Family is both a resource and a responsibility. It is endowed with all the characteristics of a small community. It has a regularity and rhythm all of its own. There are clearly defined expectations, multiple forms of life-nurturing growth, and a steady, dependable flow of privileged conversations. This woman is maximizing the fruits of loyalty. In her family there is a firm yet understood flexibility and a disciplined sense of each person's role in private and public life. The family offers a healing and wholeness that builds a capacity for compassion inside and outside the group. The tension to stay put and go forth is balanced by a keen sense of one's loyalty to the immediate and human family. Everyone is given permission to be an individual, is encouraged to befriend others, and is chosen to dignify the family by widening its embrace of life and others.

Growing virtues might be compared to planting and tending a garden. A variety of seeds/virtues are chosen according to their unique contributions to a healthy diet and wholesome living. Every seed/virtue contributes to the nourishment value of the other members of the food chain. Virtues, like plants, need more than good soil. Sun, wind, and rain maximize the plants' growth just as exercise maximizes the physical strength and the growth of virtue. Given the growth potential and life-giving power of virtues, let us look at the virtues that sustain and prolong life, those that give purpose to life, and those that amplify the enjoyment of life. Why? Because, a virtuous life is worth living.

Virtues grow in the soil of a principled life. The following virtues are commonly referred to us as the *cardinal* virtues. We know them by our human nature. Plato first formulated them, and they are also found in scripture. We grow as a person in proportion to the way we tend the seeds of these virtues. Let us call these the *foundation* virtues. They carry the weight, providing the platform, the foundation, for a virtuous life. They are justice, wisdom (prudence), courage, and moderation (self-control, temperance). There are additional liberating virtues that teach us how to use our freedom, exercise our goodness, and deal with the tyranny of selfishness. They are included among those deemed necessary as part of an ethic for healthy living.

Justice

We spend much of our life searching for people who are like us. They affirm us and take our side on issues. They are with us during our ups and downs of living, providing the security that comes from having a larger unit in society that thinks and feels like me, needs and wants like me. People we can count on supply the structure that supports our connections and convictions. They supply the substance that feeds and energizes us. This is the group that thinks, "that in all fairness" life should be the way we see it and want it.

But in truth, justice has little to do with fairness. Fairness has to do with faith in our being rewarded for our efforts; justice has to do with hope. It is about believing there is a way out of disappointment, disillusionment, and despair, and the way out does not always depend entirely on one's own doing. Justice is about transcending our tendency to only look out for ourselves. It takes moral courage to see where we do not want to look, to go where we hesitate to be involved. We have to deal with our disposition to look the other way when tempted to champion an unpopular cause and to excise ourselves when we see the magnitude of the problem. We hesitate to go where we have not been and have not been seen. Stepping across the border of our security and comfort is not easy. It is particularly daunting when we have to start by building the footbridge to cross. The difficulty is magnified when we approach the situation and see those on the other side. Often, they are people who are characterized as those who do not deserve any better. They may have been afforded the same opportunities but have been neglectful and irresponsible. They have chosen their lot in life. We may think they have forfeited our concern and help by doing little to help themselves.

These comments are really some of the longstanding explanations we use for others' indifference and ineptitude to justify our own unwillingness to cross the line that separates us. Justice is crossing the line that puts us in a place where we meet people who think otherwise. Justice looks very different to them. It is not about fairness and having their way. Justice is about acknowledging that, for one reason or another, they are in a place where they can't find their way out. The long-term solution may require dealing with the reasons. The short-term response requires seeing past our differences so we can listen to our similarities. Common ground can be found if we stand on the parcel of property that we all share and learn the reason to span our differences and share a desire to make things right.

When it comes to justice, what is right involves reaching out to those unlike us. Justice is not merely an ideal but an activity that seeks common ground through mutual understanding. Through justice, forgiveness may be an essential condition for dissolving boundaries so people can listen to one another and begin to create a new vision of life. What appears to separate us is generally ignorance of one another. What stops us is generally a road block of prejudices built to protect what we have or aspire to get. But in the end, justice errs on the side of forgiveness and generosity. Justice imagines a time and a place where everyone who is without, will receive and those who have, will give. Fellowship and brotherhood will replace estrangement. Giving and receiving meet without reservation and resistance. The self-offering is redemptive as all participate in the benefits of solidarity and peace. Through justice, there is no division and no one takes sides.

We are more likely to be forgiving if we make justice a cornerstone in our lives. Forgiveness depends upon finding common ground for building a more viable and lasting relationship. It is not about balancing rewards and punishments or it is about achieving a balance between personhood and humanity. There is a give and take which enhances and preserves the individual psyche and the collective conscience. A partnership between justice and forgiveness is both a solitary and collective act of the will. It looks to wisdom for understanding, insight and compassion.

Wisdom (prudence)

Wisdom is a many-sided prism through which we see eternal verities and the interconnectedness of all of life. On the one hand, wisdom is bordered and discrete. On the other hand, wisdom is vast and is an organic sensitivity and sensibility. Wisdom is a single direction that orients us toward a deeper imagination toward hidden levels of being, and serves to prefigure and animate truth. We are engrafted to purity and innocence, engulfed with an infatuation and gratuitousness that is life-generating, life-bearing, and life-giving. Wisdom staunchly unearths truth's inner workings and avidly pursues the broad vistas of truth's connectedness to faith, hope, and love. Wisdom is rejuvenated by truth which is at once awakened awareness, enlightened self-observation, shattered illusions, and stripped-down reality. Truth stands naked before wisdom. Disclosed, wisdom wraps truth in the blanket of humility and places truth in the maternal arms of its embrace.

Wisdom is generally tentative and cautious, not impulsive and impetuous. Gaining wisdom means that we do not leap ahead of our ability to collect, sort, and prudently raise the grains of truth collected from wisdom. Wisdom refuses to be tempted to throw the seeds of truth to the winds and hope they fall on good ground. Rather, wisdom relies upon a tranquil spirit and is not in a hurry to see results. It can wait knowing truth yields a better harvest from fallow ground.

Wisdom knows the secret of the seasons of life. It takes a kernel of truth, plows the rich soil, and sows the seed. It then respects the seasons of the year. There is no hurrying the sun or the rain for growth has its own hidden and holy cycle. There is a rhythm to life that must be respected. Wisdom does not yield its treasures without being given its due. In due time, the harvest of truth will be made ready. Wisdom looks for the signs of the harvest with anxious anticipation. Wisdom is truth brought to fruition, justice grown and harvested.

Wisdom is the raw material for all acts of justice. Thus it is also serves as a bold initiative for forgiveness. Wisdom reduces the chances of applying a double standard when forgiving oneself and forgiving others. It helps us develop habits of mind and discover blind spots in our hearts. Wisdom can be persuasive because it feeds our appetite for justice. Wisdom can be put in the service of what is practical, particularly when it tempers our tendency to construe fair and unfair in terms of having our own way. Forgiveness relies upon the understanding, insight and compassion supplied by wisdom. Without these qualities we would continue to insist we are right without regard to the facts and would defend our position without recourse to reason. Forgiveness requires coming to our senses—putting them on trial, all of them – to mediate our differences and find a defensible solution. Wisdom is a door we walk through and a window we see through so we can stand and look together.

Wisdom and justice are essentially about awareness. Both awaken us to knowing we are better than we think and thinking we can be better than we are. The awakening is the first step in a process of growing into a greater understanding and appreciation of our willingness to see, listen, and discover that we all belong to a universal principle and a common destiny. That is, we are all to love one another. We are all to be nurtured and confirmed by this truth. When truth yields to wisdom and justice yields to faith, we act in enlightened and healthy self-interest. We can use the intrinsic relationship between wisdom and truth to learn how to exchange our self-interest for the interests of others. Occasionally, we may need to step aside as an act of charity, and, at our best, we'll restrain our desire for more in order to serve the self-interest of others. In our new understanding, wisdom and justice will thrive when they depend upon one another for direction, loyalty, and courage.

Courage

We all know what it is like to be vulnerable and scared to death. No one stays immune to the thoughts or experiences of the world as a dangerous place. Courage involves an internal conflict. It depends upon believing "no one can do anything to me that I am not prepared for. I do what I have to do in spite of the doom and gloom which has me second-guessing myself."

We build part of our world with our fears that derive from our imagination working overtime when we are afraid. But when we are fearful, we have to participate in the aftermath. It matters not that what we fear is contrived more than real, we respond in similar ways. We withdraw, retreat, or hide even when the struggle is within us. We take refuge by distancing ourselves from whatever threatens our ability to take control of a situation. When the situation is unexpected, we are more prone to seek safety. Yet, often it is the expected situations, the ones we have previously experienced, that rouse the most fear. All we want is for the fear, the situation, to go away and not come back another day.

Yet only when the fear comes back do we have a chance to reintroduce ourselves to the problem and confront it with what we learned from the previous encounter. Once settled, in a calm and introspective manner, we may look within ourselves, make an inventory of our resources, and devise a way of looking at and then resolutely dealing with a similar situation later on.

Stepping out to express the courage of one's conviction is always a risk that requires a steadfast resolve to be true to oneself. Without a doubt, unforeseen consequences will arise when facing undetermined odds. Courage does not always get a hero's welcome. In fact, it can arouse suspicion and cause others to put up their guard. Breaking through the armor of resistance may take more than conviction and tenacity. Advancing around the edges of the disagreement may be the most prudent course of action. There is something less threatening about bold actions when they are not thrust at the center of the issue. Finding courageous counterpoints and places to meet where both parties can act without feeling protective opens the outer boundaries of the dispute.

Courage is generally a virtue that is built from our discoveries. The discoveries include learning about the object of our fears, coping with our limitations, and garnering the strength to get through the worst that life puts before us. Just as we take an active part in creating and/or elevating our fear, we learn to take apart what disturbs and distresses us in the face of the previous or current unknown. Courage is about learning how to take control when something threatens our ability to trust ourselves. *I can't* has to be replaced with *I must* and *I will*. One condition (I can't) is fashioned from a resolute attitude while the other (I will/I must) is forged from steadfast and decisive actions. Nothing quite like desire and determination can break the barrier between being afraid and being enough. We can all be enough because we can learn to gather, develop, and apply our interior resources on behalf of competence.

Courage is not anxious, fragile, and guarded. It means facing life's challenges in the service of an idea or an ideal. There are no limits to its reach because it stretches one's endurance and defers to no one. In the midst of controversy, courage knows when, where, and how to step in and take charge and join forces.

We can all be more than survivors in life. But that may mean throwing caution to the wind and letting go of compromise. When we face such a life situation, courage neither makes nor accepts excuses. It is the posture assumed by those who know what they stand for. Since it refuses to lie down in the face of predicaments and conflict, it does not mince words when taking on the opposition. It acts regardless of reservations after we have thoughtfully and selectively decided what life is about and how to bring it about.

When we compare cowardice and courage, we see that courage can claim the victory but it will take inner determination. Cowardice is calculating and runs from the truth. Courage cherishes the truth and runs after it. Cowardice is self-serving and fashioned from thoughts of recognition and admiration. Courage is selfless, unflinching faith in decency and the determination to live in the fullness of life. Cowardice lays down its arms and runs away from a fight for justice. Courage takes up arms and does battle to protect, advocate, and work for justice. Cowardice quits because it lacks the energy of conviction and compassion. Courage is energized by conscience and commitment. Cowardice is guarded and waits to see who is on board. Courage is brave and sets the agenda.

Courage is a virtue worthy of everyone who wants to live a principled life. One does not have to be a hero or act heroic. Courageous people do the right things for the right reasons. They also persist in defining what the right things are. They seek the truth as the basis for the right reasons. They are liberated from the fears that isolate them from others and make them strangers to themselves. Courageous people do not hesitate to be themselves and resist self-deception. Courage is the strength to trust oneself and take a chance on life.

Moderation

Everything is acceptable in moderation, say the experts on all sorts of issues. Dietitians tell us if we choose from all the food groups in proportion to our body requirements, we can expect to enjoy good health. These expectations drive our desire to feel good while eating good. We are likely to maintain a healthy diet as long as there is a reasonable correspondence between our choices, actions, and expectations. We may not particularly like the regimen or the lack of freedom to eat with abandon, but the benefits outweigh the costs. We comply with the requirements, make the associated sacrifices, and derive sufficient satisfaction to moderate our inclination to disregard the adverse consequences. In this way, we learn to manage our compulsions, learn to preside over our eating habits. We learn to refrain from eating to excess. We place limits on the amount we eat from the more appealing food groups. It is all about being sensible.

In our lives, moderation, or temperance, is not confined to our eating habits. We can also drink, work, and sleep to excess. We need to savor what is sensible and achieve a balance between doing and overdoing. Temperance challenges us to exercise good judgment, develop healthy habits, and associate with others who share this outlook and practice this virtue. Temperance helps us acquire habits of self-restraint, thereby moderating expectations, abstaining from excesses, and cultivating a measured response to what we like and want.

Moderation, or temperance, might seem like a simple approach to forgiveness, because, in some ways, temperance does nothing but listen. Yet there is something calming and refreshing about doing nothing to change a situation, only making oneself available to listen. The calm allows one to hear the whispers of soul-imparted wisdom. The refreshment lets a cool breeze pass over pent-up pools of strident emotion. Exaggeration stands still and stares out through the darkness. It cannot have its way because a flame of moderation casts its light across the divide. When we listen carefully to the approach of moderation, doubt cannot cast a spell on thoughts seeking unity and solidarity.

Still, as people, we sometimes have a difficult time trusting simplicity. Culturally, we tend toward a "more is good" mentality, a new, better, and improved approach to life. Simplicity is about subtraction while advertisements urge us to see life as addition and multiplication. There is something noble about participation in something at a very basic and unadulterated level. There is richness in simplicity. It seeks nothing for itself. Thus there is always enough of the essence and essential for everyone. There is no reason to claim more than we need because neither stinginess nor excess have a place at the table. There is no place for greed, cheating, and exploitation. There is no miserliness because sufficiency replaces scarcity as a habitual way of thinking.

Temperance then can be an invitation to imagine we are on an open pathway to undiscovered dimensions of having without possessing and indulging. We can imagine ways of living fully without confirming to a world of objects and objections. We can see the fraudulent ways we are enticed into believing that happiness is about having more rather than learning to do with less. We refuse the insistent demands to make life a way of securing things to feel secure, of doing to believe we are, and of clinging to the illusion that happiness is carving out a permanent niche for ourselves. Imagination helps us discover that nothing in life can make us secure regardless of how hard we work for it. Imagination can take us beyond ourselves and fling us past contrived satisfaction into a place that illuminates the mind and delights the heart. Imagination can cleanse us of our preoccupation with acquiring things to feel secure. Imagination can greet us with titillating surprises, marvelous good feelings, and stir us to enter a mysterious universe of possibilities. Temperance in life permits the pendulum to swing away from the illusion of certainty and toward a fusion of modest realities deeply understood and richly lived. Virtue flourishes in the soil of temperance.

Hospitality

We live in a society where people are invariably chasing some dream imposed from outside consumer forces. But we can never catch up with the mythical Jones's. They are an illusion created by a society that markets ideas and ideals dedicated to selling the products. Those "wanted" products come with a price we pay by the way we choose to use our time. We are busy making ends meet and that leaves little time for activities that don't serve our unquenchable thirst for more. Time becomes a commodity, but we feel there is just not enough of it to go around. In seeking the virtuous life, we do not want to squander the remaining time.

Hospitality is simply borrowing time by renegotiating our priorities. Some self-serving activities will relinquish some of their time in the interest of activities to serve others. Additional less-favored activities may be struck from life's agenda altogether because they lack the imperative and non-negotiable requirements of hospitality. We may have to put the squeeze on ourselves to make time for others. And we may not be able to get what is needed by having to squeeze it out of our leisure time. Like a well-spent tube of toothpaste, applying lots of pressure does not necessarily produce much substance. Hospitality can be a life-giving substance but we often feel it can exact more time than we are willing to give it. Hospitality is often a casualty when it competes with work and work-related priorities. We look upon hospitality as a bargaining chip when we gamble on life. It isn't all that essential because the winnings are generally modest and often too intangible to make a noticeable difference in the ways we live.

Some years ago I decided to make a concerted effort to involve hospitality in my life. I decided to make myself available on someone else's terms. It seemed like an ideal way to develop this virtue because I would sacrifice some control and order in favor of others' need for emergency assistance. I would have to resist the temptation to save and use time as a commodity that belonged to me. I would have to allow inconvenience to make a claim on my life.

Through this volunteer work, I have been called upon to rescue many people from the grips of hunger, from eviction, and the loss of household services. I have often found the help requested was no more important than the opportunity to talk about unexpected, untimely, and unfortunate circumstances that brought me to the people I served. Their feelings of helplessness and hopelessness drained their emotional bank account and rendered them without much energy to pull themselves up by their bootstraps. For the most part, these were people down on their luck who lacked the strength to lift themselves up. I learned life is a perilous journey for some. Each day danger lurks in the darkness of their hearts and refuses to release its hold on their desperation and despair. Hospitality is the intangible benefit of listening with an open mind and understanding heart. Help with no strings attached loosens the grip of fear and uncertainty, anger, and resignation. We are people first and help merely expresses our humanity.

I have also learned many people do not have a network of friends and relatives who can rescue them from unforeseen calamities, questionable choices, and downright irresponsibility. The reason for their plight has nothing to do with what is justifiable. When it comes to matters of hospitality, need takes precedence over all other considerations. Hospitality that begins in the heart and soul is about bringing together those who are often separated by the dark and stark realities of life. It is about strangers first finding a place to meet, greeting one another in their common humanity, and then exchanging something of value. They become the guests in one another's heart. One cannot place an exact value on the exchange. Exactness has little to do with hospitality. Matters of the heart are not normative and are, therefore, not subject to standard forms of measurement.

Hospitality is not just a neighborly exchange of give and take such as accepting an invitation and later reciprocating. In that instance, hospitality is merely satisfying a social amenity and is frequently perceived as an obligation. Both parties are able to serve the other because they have the means to measure out an appropriate response to the kindness and consideration of the other. They respond somewhat as equals with similar resources for doing so. But the <u>virtue</u> of hospitality is best learned and cultivated when one party cannot return the favor in like kind. Rather, they renounce a desire to be self-sufficient by yielding some sufficiency and depending on the good will of another. Often the one who is supposedly doing the giving is the one receiving. Scripture also reveals a realm where everything is turned upside down. Hospitality is a sure pathway to the heart by entering a sacred space and meeting one another as soulmates. The pathway is not crowded because so many people mistakenly believe hospitality is an exchange of goods when it is actually an exchange of goodness. Most people would rather supply the goods than distribute them; pay for the goods rather than pay the bill with their lives. Hospitality often requires standing in the mess and clearing away the debris. It creates a place where everyone can stand on solid ground and in solidarity with one another.

Humility

Humility is facing the truth about ourselves and understanding that we are not perfect. We will always come up short of perfection regardless of how hard we work at it. We just haven't been given enough of everything to do nor can we be everything that's required to be perfect. Yet, we would not need anyone else if we were all that is required. How lonely we would be if nothing in life lay outside our grasp. Even in small ways we would not have to depend upon others. There would be no reason to call upon another, no basis for learning to give something to another, no necessity to learn to love another. We would be self-contained and self-sufficient units. We would be a society without any other members.

To me, humility is simply being who I am. It is a place where I can find rest because I am not always out proving myself. I can accept and appreciate myself without explaining and defending myself. I do not have to be someone I am not. I can be comfortable in my own skin and little can rub me the wrong way. My estimation of myself does not depend upon the assessment of others. I do not have to be a mathematician to measure my worth and calculate my success. I am less anxious because I do not ascend and descend on an elevator where someone else pushes the buttons. Humility gives me permission to become my unique and irreplaceable self.

This does not mean we do not imagine and strive to be more. It merely means we don't have to be more to think well of ourselves. In fact, continually trying to be in charge of our lives can be an enemy of humility. Order wants to make everything fit in place so we can sit back and admire ourselves. We soon learn we can't always be in charge and make things work out the way we are convinced they should. When this happens, we become disillusioned and discontented with our condition in life. Despite doing more our lives still seem out of control. We engage in a war with our ego that will never be content as long as it is deprived of having its way. The ego exalts itself; it seduces us into believing we deserve better and that happiness is having our own way. Pride that comes from our own ego is constantly positioning itself to win. It is a posture that cannot stand up to defeat without blaming or devastating another.

The essence of humility is befriending our shortcomings. We shake hands with the other side of us. We welcome the difference between what we are and what we aspire to have or be because this gives us something to seek. We may never overcome our shortcomings, but we can learn to cope or compensate for them. Only when we accept our limitations can we truly appreciate our strengths and appropriate the contributions of others for ourselves. Humility also means accepting the limitations of others and letting both parties be comfortably at home with themselves with no need to pretend to be somebody else. Both parties can live with the truth. We are told the truth will set us free—free to live without constantly second guessing ourselves.

As we think about what humility means in our lives, we acknowledge that it is not shameful to be humble. Nor should humility make us feel guilty. We all have our faults; we all have our regrets. Acknowledging this lets us forgive ourselves and be charitable toward ourselves. Only when we are charitable can we simultaneously stand up before our limitations and bend down before our strengths. Charity brings a transformative power to our limitations but lets us also respect the fragility of our strengths. With this perspective of our personal virtues, we do not have to defend our deficiencies nor diminish our strengths. We can live comfortably inside the houses of the lives we build with stone, creating a strong foundation from virtues. Our houses have been modestly built on the solid foundation of meekness and restraint. With a virtuous foundation, our houses are unpretentiously furnished so anyone who steps inside feels welcome. No one has to apologize for humility for it carries its own credentials. Humility does not entitle us to anything. It is a form of authority that speaks for itself.

Humor

An old woman is busted for shoplifting a can of peaches. She goes to court. The judge asks how many peaches were in the can. There were four. So he gives her four days in jail and four days of community service. Quickly the woman's husband who's sitting in the courtroom raises his hand to address the judge. He says, "Your honor, she also stole a can of peas."

Absence of humor and other virtues does not make the heart grow fonder! Occasionally we may have to shoplift some time and distance to separate us from our disagreements with our own lives and those in our lives. Humor helps us look at life differently. We can get some relief from grinding our teeth and grudgingly being nice. Humor has a way of cleansing the soul as it topples our sanctimonious thoughts and cuts us down to size.

Laughter is like a magic wand waved over tension so strong it can be cut with a knife. Laughter can reduce the power of resentment, bitterness, and hostility. It is a brief excursion into a world where nothing is taken too seriously. At least momentarily, it changes one's perspective. When shared between two who stand apart, it helps them cross the threshold of a common denominator. Laughter has a way of engaging us in a picture that includes both the teller and the listener. It is almost unthinkable, even when a story produces little more than a tickle, to waste the opportunity to laugh. As one recovers from a humorous moment, something may also be recovered from a relationship gone sour. Laughter is sweetness poured over the blandness left over when there is nothing really serious to be mad about. Humor is devoid of self-righteousness and self-possession. Humor is free of smugness and superiority. It is a light-hearted, once-and-for-all pathway to forgiveness.

Humor can heal even if it is used as an indirect route to forgiveness. Humor adds a touch of playfulness to life. It makes light of our human condition. Through humor we can be caught being ridiculous without being mortified. We can participate in the absurd without feeling foolish. Laughter has a way of cutting us down to size. When we size ourselves up from this more wholesome perspective, we are less likely to be bewildered and severe with others. We are also less likely to set ourselves up for disappointment in our relationships or to dwell on our misfortunes. Life does frequently distort and make demands on our emotions and actions. But humor can keep the demands from being a constant disturbance. After all, life is what we make of it and making it with deliberate and spontaneous dashes of laughter will inoculate us against the erroneous idea and destructive tendency to believe life is so damned important that we must hold out for perfection.

A couple who were both 60 years of age were celebrating their 40th wedding anniversary. The Special Day Good Fairy came to give each of them one wish. The woman wished an all expense world-wide tour with her husband. Swoosh! She had the reservation and tickets in hand. He wished for a beautiful female companion thirty years younger. Swoosh! He was ninety years old. The wife took life and married life seriously. He took himself too seriously. The joke was on him and it was no laughing matter!

Loyalty

We like life to be predictable; we like people to be dependable; and we like to feel secure. We are more likely to feel those desires are constant when all of our information points to one conclusion and sends us off in one direction. And, when that information is discovered and disclosed by people who have a reputation for being honest, dependable and forthright, we are more likely to trust it. These are the people we regard as loyal friends and confidants. Often to be one is to know one.

Like a passport, loyalty entitles people to travel wherever they like in our lives. It certifies the bearer as one who has our trust and confidence. We need not be suspicious about their whereabouts. Regardless of where they are, we can count on them in the time of our need. They will drop everything if we need to be picked up. They will back us when we lack the backbone to defend ourselves. Loyalty is about solidarity in the face of division, doubt and uncertainty. Loyalty defines a relationship wherein two persons reside in a realm defined by similar moral claims and is rooted in common certitudes.

As we further consider loyalty, we see that loyalty is more than duty which only binds us to what is right. Loyalty makes a wider claim on our lives by claiming our identity. We cannot easily escape the claim because then we would be denying ourselves. We could not live comfortably and securely with ourselves if we abandoned the ideal or betrayed the person. Our humanity, not just our identity, is at stake. Loyalty is a way of belonging to one another. It is also a way of being there for one another when the stakes are high and a strong probability of adverse consequences exists. But often loyalty is fraught with inconvenience. It means being there when we would prefer to be somewhere else. It means my time is your time, time and time again. A handshake is a sufficient guarantee that when an occasion requires it, one person will exchange his/her freedom for another's welfare.

With loyalty as a virtue we are restless to do the right thing for the right people, often without waiting to be asked. Loyalty sees with the eyes that can detect the smallest ripples in otherwise calm waters. Loyalty does not jump in and come to the rescue. Rather, loyalty watches patiently for signs that all may not be well and only then introduces itself into the situation. Loyalty is not worried about missing out on something. Rather it is concerned about missing something that requires availability and possibly attention. Loyalty has many faces. There is generally one looking in the direction of those whose life is intertwined with ours. Loyalty is a bridge to security and happiness. It knows no boundaries for it takes up habitation in the heart of another.

Fortitude

Some people are known as persons of conviction. Regardless of what others might think of that person or withhold from him, that person stands by the principles and practices that must be defended. It takes fortitude to be consistently identified as the standard bearer for a demanding creed, a controversial issue, or an unpopular change. To be an advocate for someone living on the margins, to insist on the rights for the disenfranchised, or to refuse to capitulate to the lowest common denominator requires fortitude. Fortitude is fed by injustice and gains its strength from adversity.

Often fortitude is equated with courage. In both instances a person so deeply convinces him/herself of something that he/she will take chances others would not even consider. This person is not deterred when confronted by misfortune and hardship. He stands firm and even grows stronger when met by opposition, resistance, or ridicule. Someone with fortitude champions a cause and adversity only spurs him on. People with fortitude set their course and remain steadfast in the face of danger to life and limb. They could not live with themselves if they were to do otherwise. To be at the forefront of promoting an ideal, while possibly forfeiting popularity and power, is more than a call to duty. Fortitude means feeling duty-bound to resist the temptation to run away from controversy and instead ignore the protest and prepare to do battle against all odds.

Sometimes on our journey to forgiveness we do battle with our ego. The ego can be relentless about having its way and is rooted in developing strategies for winning the war. But to live a life of forgiveness means putting down one's weapons and letting down the defenses we've created to shield ourselves from discovering our ability and need to forgive. Learning to forgive often means learning to march to a different drummer. Regardless of the perils, the fortitude we gain will lead us in this march, in this quest to be a person open to a new way of living. Those who staunchly advocate and live forgiveness herald a heart and spirit enables them to patiently bear misfortune and refuse to let go of their vision.

Forgiveness, then, is a process rooted in fortitude and righteousness. A certain passion (fortitude) drives one to go beyond the tried and the typical and to resist the temptation to be satisfied with less than perfection. Forging our way to perfection means using our imagination to put our ability to forgive into the service of goodness and wholesomeness. We long to be made whole, to feel at home with ourselves and those dear to us. Making a home in goodness and wholesomeness requires loving convictions, kindly accommodations, and patient understanding. These are conditions fashioned from fortitude, conditions that let us see possibilities where others see dead ends and let us break through barriers that others may resist.

Gratitude

Mary Jo Leddy has written an entire book devoted to a single virtue. She begins by stating a proposition that provides the scaffold, or platform, from which to view the world and make one's choices to participate in it. She asserts "What we say with our words is so much less important than what we mean with our lives. Only our lives give weight to our words. I believe that each one of us has at least one significant word to say with our lives. This word is who we really are, who we are meant to become, our calling in this world." Think of it this way—if you could say your life with one word, what would it be? Leddy chose "gratitude" as the word that summons and shapes her life. What is it about gratitude that moves us through and beyond where we are? How does it give point and purpose to life?

Why is gratitude a better springboard to launch our lives? Couldn't an equally credible case be made for faith, patience, meekness, or joy as the essence of saying our life? We have already considered a number of other possibilities. Each virtue provides us a way to evaluate and act our lives. Each has its own idiosyncratic way of simultaneously making a demand and pointing us in a direction. Each virtue is both an invitation and a initiative. The invitation beckons, the initiative hearkens. We cannot actually achieve one without the other.

Gratitude is essentially a way of looking at what we already have. It is first and foremost about sufficiency, that is, the freedom from and the freedom for. In American culture, sufficiency is freedom from the lure of wanting and having more. It is freedom from the discontent that arises out of our "if I only had." There will always be one more thing to whet our appetites and leave us perpetually hungry. Advertising creates an insatiable desire to "have and to hold" as it sells us a romantic view of life and tries to create a marriage of convenience. Unfortunately, there is a never ending list of happily here and ever after enticements. We are not immune to the pursuit of happiness the culture places before us. We increase the size of our houses and garages to placate our purchases. When we exhaust this space, we put up sheds in our backyards and rent storage units. We occasionally have a garage sale to dispose of some of our stuff. What remains is given to Goodwill or St. Vincent de Paul. It is only a matter of time before we move and new residents will likely suffer the same fate. Sufficiency may occasionally score a victory but it is short-lived. Sufficiency is about having enough and being grateful for a scaled-down way of living. It weighs in on the side of prudence, maybe frugality, and makes no apologies for adequacy as a way of thinking and behaving.

Sufficiency and simplicity make for a good marriage. Sufficiency can generally make ends meet with one income. Simplicity can be happy with what one income can afford based on a matter of taste founded in a matter of faith. It is stretch of faith to believe that a couple can be happy and grateful with what is affordable on a single income. A couple must be prepared to yield to the temptation to increase economic options by making money a priority in life. The temptation is laced with offers of convenience, comfort, and personal well-being. This piece of equipment or device will reduce the aggravation and solve the hassle of performing this operation or task. Dedicating a small amount of time to this activity can help you achieve a zest for living. The appeal of this device or participation in this activity virtually requires very little of or from you and yet assures just what you are looking for. These situations are intended to appeal to our desire to simplify our lives while getting something more or doing something more to get there. We learn to live with the contradiction and the incongruity. Generally, the old and serviceable device will produce similar results with modest inconvenience. Generally the new fangled program doesn't do anything that can't be done using some simple variation of those practices that have stood the test of time. Gratitude is often a matter of enjoying the simple pleasures of life.

Gratitude is also about satisfaction which is not easy to come by in a consumer-oriented society. The economic machine depends upon creating perpetual dissatisfaction. It does not confine itself to what we have but what we want. It is expressed in our exasperation with friends and in-laws who do not live up to our expectations, with unfulfilling work, taxes, TV programming, the price of gasoline, the salaries of CEOs, and the church we attend. We just want more out of life than it is delivering. We do not want to take no for an answer. Yet, we find ourselves powerless and impotent when it comes to rectifying the conditions that contribute to our disillusionment and discontent. We aren't asking for the world. We just want a world that takes our complaints seriously and then makes the reasoned accommodations we have in mind. We are not asking for all that much and we believe that much of what we are asking for is reasonable and can be adjudicated with common sense.

Gratitude can liberate us from our perpetual, persistent dissatisfaction. Gratitude does not dwell on what has not been, is not now, and never will be. Rather gratitude takes its cue from a popular song of many years ago and "accentuate the positive, eliminate the negative, and don't mess with Mr. in-between."

Patience

Urgency seems to be a hallmark of our culture. We are in a hurry. We just don't have enough time on our hands to be still. Regardless of where we are going or what we are doing, we need to get there yesterday and finish it quickly. Not surprising we have become a credit/debit card economy. What we want we have to have now. Why wait for a bus when we have a car? Why wait to have sex until marriage? Why wait to have a house until we can afford one? Why wait for anything when there is nothing desirable or durable in the wait that compares with the usefulness and happiness of having what we want now? Thus we have little interest or incentive in cultivating the virtue of patience.

At times we are told to be patient and this is often good advice. We see that merits of taking our time to think before acting and spending our time more wisely. The truth of the matter is we know the importance of patience, but life is too laced with endless frustration. We either end up screaming at someone else or developing ulcers because we are screaming inside. We have no use for patience when someone pulls out in front of us or steps in the line ahead of us. We struggle to be nice and understanding. But civility, consideration, and kindness go out the window once someone pushes our button. We shed ourselves of tolerance and immediately take our pound of flesh. Or, we brood over another person's offense and let pools of resentment bubble up inside of us. We try to calm the murky and heated waters of meanness and malice but eventually these feelings spill out as irritation, ridicule, grumbling, sarcasm, contempt, cynicism, indifference, and stubbornness. We fail in our efforts to pretend everything is alright or to hide our hardened heart. We just can't discard the chance to give someone a piece of our mind or a fistful of our wrath.

Patience is learning to enter and live within the natural rhythm of life. It is greeting and ordering life without expecting to much of it and from it. Life doesn't owe us anything. Life is also not about laying huge and heavy demands on ourselves. We are more likely to be impatient when we have too much to do and too little time to do it. We have to behave in heroic proportions to wed engagement and energy. Gradually, we learn to deal patiently with one another's idiosyncrasies, to gently dismiss inconsistencies, to listen without judging, and to accept without holding the other hostage to our desire for reciprocity. Eventually we learn to celebrate one another without calculating the costs or weighing the benefits in the scales of justice. Patience is a hopeful outlook on life. Over time, everything just seems to come out even.

But sometimes we cause the frustration and it is futile to try to change us. We are either oblivious to the aggravating effects of our habits of thinking or behaving, or we righteously believe we are within my rights. Since we all share this condition and posture, it will help us to learn how to charitably accommodate ourselves to what may be offensive but not destructive and respect what passes for a reasonable assertion of one's right to be his/her own person.

That doesn't mean we will tolerate an exaggerated, excessive, or unbridled selfishness for this would be a cruel, dishonest hoax.

Patience thrives on good will. Patience is an authentic blend of reason and charity. It respects norms that enjoy wide acceptance. It gives the benefit of the doubt and weighs in on the side of leniency. Patience gives us a reason to hope. We can trust the future when we are given time to hone our expectations, mine our talents, and distribute our treasure. We don't learn many things by leaps and bounds, but rather we are, by nature, voluntary and developmental by disposition. We gradually learn how to use what we have been to know and understand, to choose and act, to become and to complete. Patience is a virtue we cultivate to accept our often half-hearted attempts to grow and to generously and graciously respect this condition in others. We honor the indomitable human spirit by giving it time to pause and discover, to plan and prepare, and to deepen and extend itself beyond the boundaries built by premature closure.

Patience is the road less traveled. It means traveling lightly to reduce aggravation and exhaustion; it means dealing with division by being of one with mind and heart; it means looking the other way when we are bent upon having our way. When we would like to tell that little child to "grow up!", patience lets us wait for someone to be ready to go on. Patience is taking the long view despite being short-sighted, understanding when we prefer to be understood, and saving someone else when we are overcome trying to save ourselves. Cultivating and practicing patience favors the grooming of oneself to be a harbinger and caretaker of hope. Patience helps us gather and dispense powers in the service of growth. We gain access to the full meaning of life, to the gratification of a life well-lived, and to the discovery of those who are available and present for us. With patience we seek to dispel hurriedness, dispel anxiety, and see beyond the momentary trials and tribulations of life.

Love

The miracles of modern medicine benefit us with better quality and longer lives. We can secure inoculations against diseases that were the scourge of previous generations. We have access to medications to minimize the effects of various ailments. And we have curative medications that restore health and enable us to live more fully.

Like a medicine, love has reserve and residual qualities used to inoculate us against loneliness, depression, and despair. Love is a potion that can equip us to fight off various afflictions when we feel out of sorts with ourselves and others. Love can be viewed as a temporary and quick fix, like a mother kissing a child's wound to make it better. Love can serve the less severe afflictions of daily living. And love can help to heal the deeper wounds, those not subject to previously tried and sure ways of dealing with pain. All the same, we have trouble talking about love because we lack the words to express its various characteristics, actions, and effects.

In our increasingly complicated world, words play an important role in isolating, designing, and describing our lives. For example, with our multiplicity of medications, each medication has a name based on the primary compounds and derivatives that make it what it is. We have Zoloft, Plavex, Lunesta, and Lipator. When I was growing up, we had aspirin, iodine, and cough syrup. One did not have to exercise much judgment to select and administer these medications. Today we are so much more scientifically sophisticated and have made tremendous progress in understanding and treating various physical, mental, and emotional problems. The precise name of a drug becomes increasingly important as science and technology continue to advance our understanding of the body and our increased desire to benefit from the latest medical breakthrough. A similar change has occurred with cars. Few tools were required to keep a six-cylinder Ford running because there weren't many parts to repair. But, today a car salesperson needs a huge vocabulary just to talk about the parts and the performance advantages of each. Words are also important when I occasionally overdo my exercise regimen, go to a physical therapist, and learn that there are hundreds of words that refer to various muscles, tendons, and ligaments. I have body parts and functions with many more names than I learned in high school biology.

Not so when it comes to talking about love. We just don't have many words to refer to and talk about what it is and means to be in love. That is not to say that love is not offered as a remedy for all kinds of physical, mental, and emotional problems. We can refer to someone who we love as honey, baby, darling, or sweetheart. We can even refer to certain physical attributes of the lover – ruby lips, strawberry blonde, passionate eyes – that supposedly capture some fact/feature of love. But when it comes to expressing loving feelings, we seem to rely upon "I love you or I adore you." We fumble miserably with our language when it comes to talking about love. Our words just don't do justice to our feelings, nor do they reveal the mystery of this beyond-friendship relationship.

Maybe love is a divine ingredient. It matters not what you mix with it, the result will always look good, taste good, and feel good. How good depends upon how much love is poured into our recipe for living. Love is always in the making of life. We really don't need many words because love is gratuitous. Love in one sense is the whole word and does not require lots of variations. Like virtue, it refers to an internal condition that requires no explanation or justification. Love is a condition of the heart that makes possible all kinds of behaviors we experience. Love is an indication that we possess a divine ingredient and are using it to recreate ourselves and others anew. Love beckons us into a place and a prescription for healthy living. We cannot begin to have a full experience of life, to experience our deepest nature as human beings, in the absence of love.

So how does one live with the biblical injunction, "Over all of these put on love"? "These" in this instance are the virtues previously treated in this chapter. First, we will talk about love as a condition rather than a virtue. Love is the condition that fashions and fortifies virtues and makes them believable. Love makes it possible to appropriate and utilize the ingredients that are blended to create a virtue. A virtue cannot even become an awareness, much less an action, without being an authentic expression of love. Virtue, like love, might be contrary to our very being. Adam and Eve rejected our original blessing and charted their own selfish course. As a result, humanity began its drift away from love by turning down the fullest expression of it. We soon learned there is nothing in life that is possible or satisfying unless it is brought to fruition by the condition we call love.

Unconditional love is a perfect expression of the relationship we yearn to experience. Unconditional love was the original and perfect expression of God's love for all of His creation. This is the love wherein the right hand does not know what the left hand is doing. An abundance of seeds of this love fall on good and bad ground. Love will always bear enough fruit to go around when selfishness, self-centeredness, and greed are removed from the equation we call life.

Today we are imperfect expressions of love. We live in a flawed condition. But, love is essential to living the virtuous life and we need it to plant and cultivate our virtues. We have all been given this divine ingredient called love but we have not woven it into the fabric of our lives.

So what are the characteristics/attributes of this divine ingredient? And why do the constituent elements matter? Our ability to live love fully enhances our ability to fully know, acquire, cultivate, and act virtuously. The limits of our virtue are determined by the limits of our loving. So how do we grow in love to maximize the essential conditions to living a virtuous life?

Earlier we noted that our love vocabulary is very limited. It is difficult to plumb the word without some target words to aim at. We will rely upon the Greeks for three expressions of love. First, there is *eros*. In Platonic philosophy eros meant the yearning of the soul for the realm of the divine. It has come to mean a romantic, passionate, and physical love. This is the sex-driven love we see acted out on our televisions and movie screens. It is a love that creates a chasm between passion and responsibility, between freedom and fidelity, and between obsession and hope.

Second, there is *philia*, which means intimate affection between personal friends. It denotes a sort of reciprocal love. Ideally it is learning to see without expectations. Both parties are content to receive whatever they get and do without expecting whatever is not offered. There is no discrepancy between two "ifs", that is "if" both parties are prepared to be free of the "ifs" (the conditions), there can be an honest acceptance of their respective histories and their sense that each is already doing the best he/she can.

Finally, *agape* refers to a love rooted in understanding and redeeming good will among people. It is purely spontaneous and not motivated by self-interest. Agape is the love of God operating in a human heart. This love makes no demands and seeks nothing for itself. Agape is sometimes referred to as "neighborly love." This love can be extended to our enemies. It is generous, forgiving, and kindhearted. Sometimes we need to stop and think about how or why this love is possible. When love is difficult I ask, "What is wrong with me? What are my defects/shortcomings in this situation?" Then I find out why my love is being withheld or corrupted by my own limitations and shortcomings. I look inward to my situation. We replace a burned out light bulb with another because the bulb cannot do anything about its current condition. Just as we do not blame a light bulb for being defective, why blame other people when their light doesn't shine or it casts a shadow on our own lives? So, too, can we step out of the darkness and become the light for others.

These visions and versions provide us with some distinguishing features of love. Together they form a three-ply cord often used as a metaphor for the bond of marriage. The strength of a three-ply cord will withstand the tension of expectations pulled in various directions, of unexpected hardships, and of the inevitable conflict when self-interest and self-sacrifice butt heads with one another.

The virtuous life cannot be known, much less lived, without love. Love does not depend on anything and does not make those who receive it dependent. Love frees both the giver and the receiver to be love itself. There is no greater life than one that loves without regard to the company it keeps or the places it visits. Often love means not doing more, but doing less. Love is often what we refuse to do. We refuse to be controlled by forces that contribute to contentiousness, criticism, and cynicism. The absence of these conditions allows love to move in and abide free of unfulfilled expectations, free of a future sculpted from what we believe would make us happy, and free from the life-defeating feelings of self-glorification and self-promotion.

Those with fruitful and fulfilling lives are filled with discovery. Discovering love in its many forms and actions is something we do for ourselves and will naturally do for others. Love is the best way to do for others what you also do for yourself.

Hope

Love captures a propensity to hope. Both love and hope are prepared to give themselves to a noble cause. Both see beyond the present situation and imagine what they can accomplish together. Let us focus on hope and hear what it offers. Hope is not so naïve as to think it can get along without love. But hope, like love, makes provisions for setbacks and failures. Hope is not easily defeated, certainly not by disillusionment or disappointment.

Hope does not wait for things to change, but sets out to bring about the change as a foundation for achieving other results. Hope is evolving, ever-changing itself, it is not a static entity but a dynamic movement. Nothing is so daunting or disastrous that hope cannot find an opening to renew or restore. Hope seeks its own livelihood and provides us with everything we need for ours.

Hope sees life like a prospector mining for gold with no guarantee that our labor will produce the sought out results. At the same time, hope understands that striking it rich will only occur with some risk or labor. But living by the gold standard puts a high price on everything. Hope will pay the price, however high, because anything worthwhile will demand more than its market share.

Hope can also be likened to a seed selected for the planting. Forgiveness turns over the soil, while hope is the seed from which intimacy sprouts. Intimacy blooms when the seeds of hope penetrate the furrows of faith and love drenches them with water and light. Only when the soil is opened to the potential for new life can hope be brought to fruition.

Just as the blossom must die before the seed can bear new life, so we must die to hatred and fear before faith and love can release the new life. As the new life emerges, hope is the promise of a good yield. Hope harvests the fruits of love's labor and faith's endurance. The investment of loving faithfulness to the seeds of forgiveness produce ten fold, a hundred-fold. There is no limit to hope and to those who seek it lovingly and faithfully.

But you would not plant the seed of good intentions without preparing the soil. So it is with forgiveness. We are the soil and we must prepare ourselves to accept the seed of forgiveness. Otherwise the seed will fall on soil hostile to growth. While readying the soil is hard work, hope is always willing to go to work in our lives. We merely direct hope to serve our purposes. When our purpose is to grow intimate relationships, hope releases an enormous energy for good. Labors of hope are not uncommon among people who strive to be one with and for one another.

The seed requires nurturing because weeds can smother the seeds of good intentions. Thus faithfulness to good intentions requires an ongoing commitment to cultivate the soil. We can become negligent and permit the weeds of dissension to return. Soon plant growth is strangled by the lack of sunlight or is competing for water and other nutrients. What once started to be a plant worthy of us soon becomes one of a small yield. The yield may not be sufficient to energize the efforts that intimacy requires; it is essential to be faithful to love's plantings.

As plants spring forth from the ground, we begin to sense the possibilities. We know the outcome is still subject to a favorable climate and our commitment to our investment. Yet, hope abounds when we merge our efforts with God's providence. Hope springs eternal when the eternal One, for whom intimacy is the ultimate good, enters our acts of forgiveness.

When God enters the equation, so does grace. All the elements for goodness take their proper place. We stand in awe of our capacity to hope, to become a new creation as we permit ourselves to trust unselfish motives. While living and hoping beyond self-serving motives is demanding, it is not impossible. Motives infused with grace transcend obligation and duty as grace transforms our motives into acts of emancipation.

Hope takes us down the road to freedom. Hope is looking toward a future that makes light of the past. We have met the darkness of evil and wickedness and have refused to be conquered by it. The darkness of bitterness and revenge has been dispelled by compassion and light. We see prospects where there were problems. We embrace a vision of how things could and ought to be.

Hope is an attitude grounded in a spirit of celebration that disposes us to take a chance on living. A collective purpose emerges as we expand the universe of possibilities and include others in the quest. A collective optimism energizes movements toward reconciliation and reciprocity. Skepticism and cynicism cannot survive when people believe in something better and refuse to accept anything less. Until we find ourselves guilty of promoting alienation, we will not seek union. And until we actively seek union, we will be excluding God from part of our life.

Hopefulness is a choice that springs from our deepest longing to be connected to something larger than ourselves. It is a search for communion that feeds our hunger for wholeness. Hope is always the promise of something better; it is believing in the outcome. Hope is actively seeking something just beyond our grasp. It is not misplaced optimism, but rather imagining the realization of our expectations. Hopefulness is small triumphs along the way of the human spirit that lead to godliness.

Above all, hope is the foundation for conversion. Forgiveness then is the penultimate act of conversion that recreates, fashions, and fortifies new expectations. Like new creations, two persons see what has been unseen, hear what has been unheard, and feel what has been unfelt. Reborn through the spirit of forgiveness, they stand at the threshold of new life.

Like hope, conversion is an attitude that removes contingencies in the interest of solidarity. More important than getting even, is getting it together. More important than getting your way, is getting out of the way. More important than having the last say is being the way.

Conversion is also a surrender to being held hostage to negative feelings and behaviors. Conversion frees us from the burden of self-inflicted wounds. No longer are we bent over and dragged down by incapacitating desires for revenge. Renewed, life looks better, feels better. Now there is reason to lift your head and look down the road ahead to a promising future. You have made friends with yourself and are ready as never before to extend the hand of friendship to others.

Friendship

In the end, life is about making good friends. It is a matter of keeping displeasures and disappointments of life from coming between you and something more life-revealing and life-giving. Although the past often insists on telling us what we are not, life need not be about dwelling excessively on the past. If it is, we only think of our failures, our limitations and our long-suffering. In my case, and hopefully in yours, I am satisfied I have used the past to make friends with myself. I can cherish where I have been and feel optimistic about where I am going. I am not obsessed with changing myself. I get along just fine with myself. Others note my healthy outlook and want to be my friend as well. Although I cannot say I have arrived, I am also not intent upon getting to somewhere else. I can face myself with joy and present a happy face to the world.

We need to keep our mental and emotional selves open to accepting who we are. We need to keep our thoughts in shape to reach the end goal of self-acceptance and forgiveness. But, we are not body builders. We are one-day-at-a-time esteem builders. We work with what we have and can learn to look at life with fascination and be prepared to be surprised. There is generally something more than we are seeing and feeling right now. Being available to the moment is the first step we take toward learning to take delight in ourselves.

Once we learn to keep in step with the now, we can dance with life all around us. When we are friends with ourselves we are ready to make friends with someone else. But there is some risk involved. There is no assurance we will get what we are looking for, hoping for. We may not get the ideal partner in the dance of life. However, when we concentrate on being the good partner, we are more likely to be satisfied with the excursions into the unknown. We discover something about our own ability to be a friend which cannot happen if we remain alone with our thoughts and our fears.

Making friends with oneself is more an attitude than a course of action. We come to the attitude with some ideas about what it takes to be a friend. We are like a good cook who starts with a recipe but gradually learns to add a little of this and a little of that. No one else can get the same results adhering to the recipe nor can they ever duplicate a pinch of that and a shake of this. We begin to make friends with ourselves by following a recipe that describes some idea of what we want as a result. We start by relying on what our culture has taught us about making and building friendships. But learning to be friends with oneself eventually is about putting one's personal touch on the outcome.

The outcome has to be something that uniquely expresses what we have been given as ingredients and worked into our recipe for living.

This final chapter has been devoted to the virtues that have enduring value. These cardinal virtues of justice, wisdom, courage, and moderation are fortified and enriched by hospitality, humility, humor, loyalty, fortitude, gratitude, patience, and friendship, with love as the capstone. All together they lead us to a place where others would like to come. Upon their arrival, others will not only find someone who knows how to be a friend, but someone who has come to value him/herself as a friend. We cannot offer to be for someone else what we cannot give and do for ourselves. Friendship is always an ongoing and evolving relationship. We are at once friends while making friends. We never cease to improve upon the way we look and feel to ourselves, look and feel to others. Becoming friends with one another involves dynamic imagination and appreciation. One person supplies interest and initiative, while the other offers affirmation and gratitude. We feel confident and capable, settled and secure. We quit trying to be someone we are not. We live life looking forward and the view is wonderful when we stand on a platform built with gratitude.

A purposeful and fulfilling life originates in the company of others and expresses its fruitfulness in that way. As social beings, we are starving to achieve a satisfying balance between dependence on others and our own independence. At once we need one another and at once we only need ourselves. Learning to live comfortably in both conditions requires a lifetime of making choices, appropriating something worth knowing, claiming responsibility for what we have learned, and going forward with a more complete sense of self and the world about us. Although we will never be complete, we should see wholeness as challenge worthy of us. We learn to cherish and revere ourselves and others as noble creations. We dignify our relationships with honesty and trust. We do what we can to shake hands and invite these qualities to make their claim on us. Each day life raises the curtain when we come on stage and become part of the drama. Some days we are the hero, other days the villain. Most of the time we are merely a character actor aspiring to make our contributions to the performance. Regardless of the role we are called upon to deliver, without doing our part, others will be unable to excel at theirs.

Friendship, in varying degrees, values everyone else. Yet, it never loses sight of the axiom, you cannot have a friend unless you are one. You are one by learning to be friends with yourself. You cannot be any better to others than you are to yourself. Begin each day getting out of bed, putting your feet on the floor, stand in the presence of your best self and saying, "How could the day live without me? How could I live with myself if I did not use this day to be myself and to help others be themselves? After all, friendliness is next to godliness." When the final snapshot is taken of you, who among the living and the dead will be included in the picture?

Footnote:
Recently I reread a poem, *The Dash* by Linda Ellis. She refers to the dash as a 'little line' on a tombstone between the birth and death dates. She writes about the ways we might spend our time between these two dates. We are urged to think about what matters in life and is worth the expenditure of our years. She defers to understanding, appreciating, and responding lovingly to the people in our lives. She concludes by referring to our eulogies as pinpointing the way we spent our life. She wonders whether we will be proud of what is said about us—how we spent our dash.

Comment:
We live between the date of our birth and the date of our death. Generally, we see our earthly life as the beginning and the other as the end. But between the beginning and the end is a lifetime to be lived. For some, a lifetime was not enough. They leave behind much undone. Time was a friend to the very end. For others, a lifetime was too much. They failed to discover and cherish life. Time was an enemy from beginning to end.

Whether time is a friend or an enemy depends upon how one lives the dash. This final chapter described the character and characteristics of those who successfully and satisfyingly live the dash. The dash represents the ascending and descending events, the ups and downs of their lives. Yes, and the ordinariness and daily-ness of life when everything is rather plain and simple, not dull and dreary, but those reclusive days when we settle in and just ride the waves.

Somewhere all of this forgiveness and reconciliation make their claim on us. They are also part of the dash. They span the lifetime of those who value relationships and build a lifetime from and around them. Above everything else, relationships have their good and bad times. Many days we coast and take one another for granted. Friendships are like that. It is difficult to name our friends as having a beginning and an end. They actually transform and transcend the dash. This is particularly true when we spend the dash rather than banking on using it tomorrow.

Bibliography

Al-Mabuk, R.H., Dedrick, C.V., & Vanderah, K.M. (1998). Attribution retraining in forgiveness therapy. *Journal of Family Psychotherapy*, 9(1), 11-30.

Al-Mabuk, R.H., & Downs, W.R. (1996). Forgiveness therapy with parents of adolescent suicide victims. *Journal of Family Psychotherapy*, 7, 21-39.

Al-Mabuk, R.H., Enright, R.D., & Cardis, P. (1995). Forgiveness education with parentally love-deprived college students. *Journal of Moral Education*, 24(5), 423-444.

Al-Mabuk, R.H. (1990). *The commitment to forgive in parentally love-deprived college students.* Doctoral dissertation, University of Wisconsin-Madison, 1990. Dissertation Abstracts International-A 51(100, 1991, p. 3361).

Arendt, H. (1958). *The Human Condition.* Chicago, ILL: The University of Chicago Press.

Augsburger, D. ((2000). Five steps to interpersonal forgiveness and restored relationships. http://Jmm.aaa.net.au/articles/16906.htm

Bar-Siman-Tov, Y. (2004). *From conflict to reconciliation.* New York, NY: Oxford University Press.

Barreca, R. (1995). *Sweet revenge.* New York, NY: Berkley Books.

Bhikkhu, T. (2004). *Reconciliation, right & wrong.* Retrieved on (6/10/2006) www.accesstoinsight.org.

Bies, R.J., & Tripp, T. M. (2004). The study of revenge in the workplace: Conceptual, ideological, and ethical issues. In Fox, S. & Spencer, P.E. (Eds.), *Counterproductive workplace behavior: an integration of both actor and recipient perspectives on causes and consequences.* Washington, D.C.: APA Press.

Boese, P. (2006). *Relationships.* Retrieved on www.worldofquotes.com/relationships/Index.html.

Cardis, P. (1993). *The Psychology and measurement of revenge.* An unpublished thesis, University of Northern Iowa, Cedar Falls, Iowa.

Cose, E. (2004). *Bone to pick: Of forgiveness, reconciliation, reparation, and revenge.* New York, NY: Atria Books.

Crossin, J. W. (1998). *Walking In Virtue.* Mahwah, NJ: Paulist Press

Davis, L. (2002). *I thought we'd never speak again: The road from estrangement to reconciliation.* New York, NY: HarperCollins.

Droll, D.M. (1984). *Forgiveness: Theory and Research.* A doctoral dissertation, University of Nevada, Reno.

Donnelly, D. (1984). Forgiveness and recidivism. *Pastoral Psychology,* 15(1), 15-24.

Engel, B. (2001). *The power of apology: Healing steps to transform all your relationships.* New York, NY: John Wiley & Sons.

Enright, R.D. (2001). *Forgiveness is a choice: A step-by-step process of resolving anger and restoring hope.* Washington, D.C.: American Psychological Association.

Enright, R.D. & Fitzgibbons, R.P. (2000). *Helping clients forgive: An empirical guide for resolving anger and restoring hope.* Washington, D.C.: American Psychological Association.

Enright, R.D. & North, J. (1998). *Exploring forgiveness.* Madison, WI: The University of Wisconsin Press.

Enright, R.D., and the Human Development Study Group. (1991). The moral development of forgiveness. In *Handbook of moral behavior and development,* ed. W. Kurtines and J. Gewirtz, Vol. 1, 123-152. Hillsdale, N.J.: Erlbaum.

Enright, R.D., Gassin, E.A., & Wu, C. (1992). Forgiveness: A developmental view. *Journal of Moral Education 21(2), 99-114.*

Enright, R.d., Santos, M., & Al-Mabuk, R.H. (1987). The adolescent as forgiver. *Journal of Adolescence,* 12, 95-110.

Fincham, F.D. (2000). The kiss of the porcupines: from attributing responsibility to forgiving. *Personal Relationships,* 7, 1-23.

Fincham, F.D.& Beach, S.R. (2002). Forgiveness: Toward a public health approach to intervention. In J.H. Harvey & A.E. Wenzel (Eds.), *A Clinician's guide to maintaining and enhancing close relationships.* (pp. 277-300). New Jersey: Erlbaum.

Fincham, F.D. & Beach, S.R. (2002). Forgiveness in marriage: Implications for psychological aggression and constructive communication. *Personal Relationships,* 9, 239-251.

Folger, J.P., Poole, M.S., & Stutman, R.K. (2001). *Working through conflict: Strategies for relationships, groups, and organizations.* New York, NY: Longman.

Freedman, S.R. (1995). *Forgiveness as an educational intervention goal with incest survivors.* Doctoral dissertation, University of Wisconsin-Madison. Dissertation Abstracts International-B 55(07), p. 3034.

Freedman, S.R., & Enright, R.D. (1996). Forgiveness as an intervention goal with incest survivors. *Journal of Consulting and Clinical Psychology* 64:983-992.

Fromm, E. (1983). *The art of loving.* New York, NY: Harper.

Glasser, W. (1984). *Control Theory: A New explanation of how we control our lives.* New York, NY: Harper & Row.

Hamber, B. & Kelly, G. (2004, September). A working definition of reconciliation. A paper presented by Democratic Dialogue, Belfast, Ireland.

Hargrave, T.D. (1994). *Families and forgiveness: Healing wounds in the intergenerational family.* New York: NY: Brunner/Mazel Publishers

Hart, H.L.A. (1968). Prolegomenon to the principles of punishment. In H.L.A. Hart (Ed.), *Punishment and Responsibility.*

Heider, F. (1958). *The psychology of interpersonal relations.* New York: Wiley.

Keenan, J. F. (1996). *Virtues for Ordinary Christians.* Kansas City, MO: Sheed & Ward

Kelly, G. & Hamber, B. (2004, June). Coherent, contested or confused? Views on reconciliation in Northern Ireland. A paper presented at "Reconciliation: Rhetoric or Relevance?" A roundtable discussion on concepts and practices of reconciliation, Belfast, Ireland.

Bibliography

Kiel, D. (1986, February). I am learning how to forgive. *Decisions*, 12-13.

Kreeft, P. (1992). *Back to Virtue.* San Francisco, CA: Ignatius Press

Leddy, M. J. (2002). *Radical Gratitude.* Maryknoll, NY: Orbis Books

Maslow, A. H. (1943). A theory of human motivation. *Psychological Review,* 50(4), 370-396.

Mayeroff, M. (1971). *On caring.* New York, NY: Harper-Collins.

McCullough, M., Worthington, E.L., & Rachal, K. (1997). Interpersonal forgiving in close relationships. *Journal of Personality & Social Psychology,* 73 (2), 321-336.

McCullough, M.E. (2000). Forgiveness as a human strength: Theory, measurement, and links to well-being. *Journal of Social and Clinical Psychology,* 19, 43-55.

McCullough, M.E. (2001). Forgiveness: Who does it and how do they do it? *Current Directions in Psychological Science,* 10, 194-197.

McCullough, M.E., Bellah, C.G., Kilpatrick, S.D., & Johnson, J.L. (2001). Vengefulness: Relationships with forgiveness, rumination, well-being, and the Big Five. *Personality and Social Psychology Bulletin,* 27, 601-610.

Muller, W. (1999). *Sabbath: Restoring the sacred rhythm of rest.* New York, NY: Bantam Books.

Nelson, M.B. (2000). *The unburdened heart: Five keys to forgiveness and freedom.* NewYork:NY: HarperCollins.

Nietzsche, F.W. (1887). *The genealogy of morals*. (P. Watson translation). London: S.P.C.K.

Robinson, D. (2006). *The top ten steps to forgiveness. Retrieved on (6/25/2006).* www.topten.org.

Rogers, C.R. (1975). *On becoming a person.* Boston: Houghton Mifflin.

Rohr, R. (1992). *Simplicity: The Art of Living.* New York, NY: Crossroad.

Rohlheiser, R. (1999). *The Holy Longing: The search for a Christian spirituality.* New York, NY: Doubleday.

Rolheiser, R. (2005). *Forgotten Among the Lilies: Learning to love beyond our fears.* New York, NY: Doubleday.

Ross, M.H. (2004). Rituals & the politics of reconciliation. In Yaacov Bar-Simon-Tov Ed. (*From conflict resolution to reconciliation*). New York, NY: Oxford University Press.

Schell, D.W. (1990). *Getting bitter or getting better: Choosing forgiveness for your own good.* St. Meinrad, IN: Abbey Press.

Simon, S.B. & Simon, S. (1990). *Forgiveness: How to make peace with your past and get on with your life.* New York, NY: Warner Books.

Smedes, L. (1996). *Forgive and forget: Healing the wounds we don't deserve.* New York, NY: Harpr Collins.

Soyinka, W. (1999). *The burden of memory, the muse of forgiveness.* New York, NY: Oxford University Press.

Stuckless, N., & Goranson, R. (1994). A selected bibliography of literature on revenge. *Psychological Reports 75*, 803-811.

Stuckless, N. & Goranson, R. (1992). The Vengeance Scale: Development of a measure of attitudes toward revenge. *Journal of Social Behavior and Personality*, 7(1), 25-42.

Sulmasy, D.P. & Conley, J.J. (2000, October). At Wit's end: Dignity, forgiveness, and the care of the dying. A paper presented at the First International Symposium on Geriatric Palliative Care, Beth Israel Hospital, New York, NY.

Swenson, DX. (2002). The Ouroboros effect: The revenge effects of unintended consequences. www.css.edu/users/dswenson/web/REVENGE.HTM

Tavuchis, N. (1991). Mea Culpa: *A Sociology of apology and reconciliation*. Stanford, CA: Stanford University Press.

Wadell, P. J. (2002). *Becoming Friends: Workings, Justice and the Practice of Christian Friendship.* Grand Rapids, MI: Press

Werman, D. (1993). Edgar Allan Poe, James Ensor, and the psychology of revenge. *Annals of Psychoanalysis*, 21, 301-314.

Westermarck, E. (1932). *Ethical relativity.* New York: Hartcourt, Brace.

Williams, C. (2001). *With All We Have Why Aren't We satisfied?* Notre Dame, IN: Sorin Books.

Worthington, E.L. (2003). *Forgiving and reconciling.* Downers Grove, ILL: Intervarsity Books.

Worthington, E.L. (2005). *Handbook of forgiveness.* New York: Routledge.

Wright, W. M. (1997). Wisdom of the mothers. *Weavings, XII* (4), 6-18.

Authors' Biographies

Dr. Radhi Al-Mabuk has been interested in the research, theory, and educational and therapeutic applications of forgiveness ever since he started his doctoral program in 1984. His doctoral dissertation, completed under the wise and patient guidance of Professor Enright at the University of Wisconsin at Madison, dealt with the application of a forgiveness education program with parentally love-deprived late adolescents. Al-Mabuk has presented on the topic of forgiveness locally, nationally, and internationally, and was featured on CBS in a two-part program focusing on what forgiveness is and how to forgive. He continues to reflect on the healing and therapeutic power of forgiveness and to study factors associated with forgiveness, un-forgiveness, and reconciliation, as well as the dynamics of revenge.

Al-Mabuk has been at the University of Northern Iowa since 1990, where he is a professor of education. In addition to research, he teaches classes in the areas of human development, learning, and assessment. He and his wife are residents of Cedar Falls, Iowa, during the academic year, and spend their summers in Lutsen, Minnesota, where they enjoy hiking, river walking, kayaking, and fishing.

Dr. Len Froyen is emeritus professor of educational psychology at the University of Northern Iowa, where he taught courses in learning and developmental psychology. He is also a permanent deacon at St. Stephen the Witness Catholic Student Center in Cedar Falls, Iowa. He has served as a mentor for couples preparing for marriage and a counselor for persons in troubled marriages. In these instances, his counsel is rooted in contemplative Christian spirituality and incrementally directed problem solving.

His interest in forgiveness is an outgrowth of advanced study in counseling psychology and his work with students seeking help with distressing relationship situations. Froyen's decision to write about forgiveness was sparked and supported by his colleague and co-author, Radhi Al-Mabuk. During the writing of this book, Froyen and Al-Mabuk became friends. "Radhi generously approved of my ideas, gently forgave my idiosyncrasies, and patiently permitted me to initiate wide-ranging conversations. He fostered my desire to write with simple and introspective clarity," said Froyen, who is also the author of *Gratitude: Affirming One Another Through Stories,* published by Parkhurst Brothers Publishing in 2013.

Made in the USA
Columbia, SC
09 April 2018